# Wakaru: A Foreigner's Guide to Navigating Japanese Workplace and Corporate Culture

Danny McCain

Published by Nihon Corporate Circle, 2024.

WAKARU: A FOREIGNER'S GUIDE TO NAVIGATING JAPANESE WORKPLACE AND CORPORATE CULTURE

**First edition. November 2, 2024.**



ISBN: 979-8227541987

Written by Danny McCain.

# Table of Contents

# Introduction

Imagine walking into a room where every eye glances in your direction, not with open curiosity, but with the slightest shift in expression, barely perceptible yet powerful enough to convey: *Do you understand?* It's not always easy for foreigners to grasp the Japanese way of work, especially when cultural expectations come unspoken and deeply ingrained. Yet, understanding the nuances of Japanese workplace culture can be a game-changer.

From the Meiji Restoration's drive for modernisation to post-WWII influences, Japan has a long history of adopting and adapting foreign practices, often in surprising ways. The famous image of General Douglas MacArthur standing next to Emperor Showa symbolises this paradox well: while bowing to foreign authority when necessary, Japan also shields a core identity, steeped in pride and hierarchy, that can be a challenge to decipher. This book is for the "outsiders"—the Western executives, the foreign talent, the curious traveller—who want to go beyond scratching the surface and truly understand how to navigate Japan's corporate and social spheres.

In the following pages, you'll find a blend of history, humour, practical advice, and real-life examples to help you "get along" with Japan on its own terms. This book isn't here to teach you how to bow, but rather when to stand firm—and when to politely nod along. If you're ready to look past the calm, orderly surface and into the intricate social choreography that underpins Japan's workplace culture, then *Wakaru* is for you.

# Part 1: Historical Context – From Meiji Modernisation to the American Influence Post-WWII

# Chapter 1: The Meiji Restoration and Japan's Rapid Modernisation

## Japan Before the Meiji Restoration: Isolation and Tradition

Before the dramatic reforms of the Meiji period, Japan was a world largely closed off from outside influence. For over 200 years, during what's known as the Edo period, the country maintained a policy of strict isolationism, called *sakoku*, under the Tokugawa shogunate. This was a Japan defined by a rigid caste system, deep-rooted Confucian values, and a strict adherence to traditional roles and social norms. Such a system wasn't merely about hierarchy; it was a meticulously structured society where everyone from the samurai to the peasants knew their place and duty. Foreign influence was minimal, limited to a handful of Dutch and Chinese traders on the island of Dejima, just off the coast of Nagasaki.

This era's hallmark was stability—granted at the cost of innovation. The Japanese people largely adhered to their local customs, untouched by Western technologies, philosophies, or societal shifts. To understand the Meiji Restoration, we must first understand this context of isolation, which would eventually make Japan's rapid transformation so dramatic. By the mid-19th century, however, the world was changing at an unprecedented rate. Industrialisation had taken root in the West, with countries like Great Britain, France, and the United States reaping the benefits of new technology, mass production, and scientific advancement. This age of expansion soon brought Western ships to

Japan's shores, igniting a chain reaction that would reshape the island nation in ways few could have imagined.

During this period of isolation, Japan's economy, political system, and social structure all revolved around a delicate balance. The shogunate, or military government, had absolute control, with the emperor serving more as a figurehead than a ruling monarch. Samurai, the warrior class, sat atop the social pyramid, followed by farmers, artisans, and merchants. Samurai adhered to a strict code of honour known as *bushido*, which emphasised loyalty, bravery, and a disciplined way of life. Although they held status and respect, the samurai often lived under modest means, with wealth often considered less important than honour.

Below the samurai class were the farmers, who produced rice, the nation's primary currency and food staple. Farmers were respected for their role in sustaining society but were heavily taxed and largely at the mercy of the ruling class. Artisans and craftsmen occupied the third tier, contributing to Japan's rich cultural landscape with their creations, from pottery to textiles. At the bottom of the hierarchy were the merchants, whose dealings in money and goods were seen as somewhat dishonourable in a Confucian society that prized production over trade. Ironically, despite their low social standing, many merchants amassed significant wealth, quietly disrupting traditional values with an emerging focus on commerce.

Under this social framework, Japan enjoyed relative peace and order, yet it was stagnant and, in some ways, insulated from global progress. It's important to note that Japan's isolation was not an indication of ignorance or indifference to the outside world. Japanese scholars kept a close eye on developments in China, Korea, and even Europe through a discipline known as *rangaku*, or "Dutch learning." In a controlled way, the Japanese studied Western science, medicine, and technology, albeit without fully integrating these advancements into society. Through this limited exposure, the Japanese were aware of Western military prowess and technological sophistication, and the ruling class understood that Japan's archaic systems might not withstand a direct confrontation with the West.

But the isolation was also a point of pride. Japan was free from the cultural upheavals seen in other parts of Asia under colonial influence. They were autonomous, untouched by foreign rule, and self-sustaining. The Japanese deeply valued their traditions, which they saw as a stabilising force. Buddhism, Shintoism, and Confucian ideals formed the philosophical backbone of society. To be Japanese was to understand and respect the ways of one's ancestors, to follow the rituals and social codes that had kept the nation stable for centuries. In this way, isolation was not just a political stance but a cultural one, a preservation of a unique identity.

Yet, by the mid-1800s, cracks were appearing in this well-ordered system. The Tokugawa shogunate faced internal pressure from samurai who were frustrated with economic hardship, peasant uprisings due to heavy taxation, and the rising influence of wealthy merchants who quietly challenged the social order. The power of the shogunate itself began to weaken, as regional leaders, or *daimyo*, grew increasingly independent, challenging the centralised rule. Japan's stability rested on a precarious foundation, one that was vulnerable to external forces.

The Western colonial powers, meanwhile, were increasingly keen on expanding their markets and influence in East Asia. Commodore Matthew Perry's arrival in 1853, with his "black ships," symbolised this shift. Perry's show of military power was a stark reminder of Japan's vulnerability and the technological disparity between East and West. The Americans demanded Japan open its ports to trade, and the threat of force loomed large over the negotiations. For Japan, the choice was stark: open up or face invasion. Perry's presence was a harbinger of a new world order, one that Japan could no longer ignore.

The forced signing of the Treaty of Kanagawa in 1854 marked the beginning of the end for Japan's isolation. Western influence, once carefully managed, now surged through Japan's borders, challenging the established order and forcing the country to confront its own vulnerabilities. The samurai class, which had enjoyed centuries of prestige, now faced a new reality. They were no longer the ultimate defenders of a closed Japan; instead, they had to adapt or risk becoming obsolete in a rapidly modernising world. This moment catalysed what would soon become the Meiji Restoration, a radical overhaul of Japanese society aimed at closing the technological and military gap with the West.

Japan's willingness to adopt Western methods—while retaining a distinctly Japanese core—would prove instrumental in its journey towards modernity. In the coming decades, the nation would undergo a transformation that was unprecedented in both scope and speed. The end of isolation marked not only a shift in Japan's relationship with the outside world but also a deep internal restructuring. It was a time when old traditions were challenged, new identities forged, and Japan began its march towards becoming a formidable global power. Understanding this foundational shift is key to grasping the intricate layers of Japanese corporate and social hierarchy that persist even today.

## The Arrival of Commodore Perry and the Push to Modernise

IN THE MID-19TH CENTURY, as Western nations expanded their influence across the globe, Japan remained a largely secluded, agrarian society. While much of Asia fell under European colonial rule, Japan's strategic decision to limit foreign influence allowed it to maintain a unique cultural and political independence. But with the arrival of Commodore Matthew Perry and his squadron of "black ships" in 1853, Japan's self-imposed isolation was about to come to an abrupt end. Perry's mission, sanctioned by the United States government, was to open Japan's ports to American trade. Yet, this mission went beyond mere commerce; it represented a turning point, a forced confrontation with the technological might of the West that exposed Japan's vulnerabilities.

When Perry's fleet sailed into Edo Bay (modern-day Tokyo Bay), the impact was immediate and unsettling. The sight of the massive, steam-powered ships left an indelible impression on the Japanese, who were accustomed to smaller, wind-driven vessels. The Japanese had witnessed Western technology through limited contact with the Dutch at Dejima, but the power and scale of Perry's fleet underscored the gap between Japan's feudal systems and the industrialised West. Perry's ships were not just vessels of trade—they were symbols of Western military dominance and a stark reminder of Japan's inability to defend itself against a foreign power. Perry's insistence on diplomacy, backed by the threat of force, placed Japan in an impossible position: either open its doors willingly or face military aggression.

Perry's arrival was no coincidence. The United States, driven by the concept of Manifest Destiny and the need for new markets, saw Japan as an ideal trading partner in East Asia. With the success of China's forced opening under British influence, the Americans believed Japan's time had come. The Treaty of Kanagawa, signed in 1854, marked the official end of Japan's isolation and initiated a new chapter in its history. This treaty opened two Japanese ports to American vessels and established a U.S. consulate in Japan, breaking the long-held *sakoku* policy. This agreement was the first of several "unequal treaties" that would soon follow with other Western powers, each imposing economic and legal concessions on Japan that favoured the foreign signatories.

The impact of Perry's visit and the subsequent treaties on Japan's leadership was profound. The shogunate, once the unchallenged ruling power, faced criticism for succumbing to foreign demands. Many in Japan viewed these concessions as humiliating, an affront to national pride. This sense of vulnerability exposed the cracks in the Tokugawa shogunate's authority and catalysed a national debate on Japan's future. The samurai class, traditionally the backbone of Japanese society, felt especially threatened. Here was a foreign power, once considered inferior, now dictating terms to Japan. The shogunate's perceived failure to protect Japan's sovereignty led to mounting calls for reform and a shift in power away from the ruling shogunate to the emperor.

This period of national soul-searching led to a fervent discussion about Japan's path forward. Intellectuals, officials, and samurai began to advocate for a programme of modernisation, arguing that Japan needed to adopt Western technologies, institutions, and even military tactics if it hoped to defend itself and maintain independence. This was not an easy transition, as it meant abandoning or significantly modifying many of the traditions that had defined Japanese life for centuries. But the Japanese people were pragmatic; they saw the writing on the wall. The lesson was clear: either adapt to the global order or risk subjugation.

One of the most notable figures of this movement was Yoshida Shoin, a samurai intellectual who became a fierce advocate for modernisation. Yoshida's teachings promoted the idea that Japan must learn from the West without sacrificing its national essence. He argued that adopting Western science and technology was not a betrayal of Japanese identity but rather a necessary step to secure Japan's sovereignty. His ideas gained traction, particularly among young samurai, and set the stage for the Meiji Restoration. The notion of "Eastern ethics, Western science" became a guiding philosophy, blending respect for Japanese traditions with the practical benefits of Western innovation.

By the time of the Meiji Restoration in 1868, Japan was ready to embark on a path of rapid modernisation, seeking to close the technological and military gap exposed by Perry's arrival. This drive to modernise was all-encompassing, affecting every aspect of Japanese life. Educational systems were restructured, military ranks standardised, and Western industrial methods embraced. In less than half a century, Japan transformed from a feudal society to a burgeoning industrial power, an unprecedented feat that astonished Western observers. But this transformation was not simply a process of imitation; Japan meticulously adapted foreign practices to fit its unique cultural framework, retaining a sense of national identity even as it absorbed Western technology and knowledge.

The impact of Perry's arrival and the treaties that followed cannot be overstated. They served as both a catalyst for change and a cautionary tale. Perry's visit demonstrated the power of Western imperialism and the ruthlessness with which it was pursued. For Japan, these lessons went beyond economics and diplomacy; they shaped a national mindset that remains relevant in modern Japan. The emphasis on vigilance, adaptability, and the careful negotiation of foreign influence has become part of Japan's cultural DNA. Even today, Japan approaches globalisation with a unique blend of openness and caution, a legacy of its forced opening in the 1850s.

In understanding Japan's corporate and workplace culture, the lessons of Perry's visit echo through the ages. The Japanese learned to respect strength, particularly when wielded with restraint, and to navigate external pressures without compromising core values. In many ways, Japan's approach to foreign influence in the workplace mirrors its historical stance: engage with the outside world when necessary, adapt and innovate internally, but always on Japan's terms. This balancing act, born out of necessity in the mid-19th century, laid the foundation for the complex, hierarchical, and uniquely Japanese corporate culture that outsiders encounter today.

# The Overhaul: Meiji-Era Reforms and the Rise of Industrial Japan

THE MEIJI RESTORATION of 1868 marked a complete overhaul of Japanese society. After centuries of feudal rule, Japan embarked on an ambitious project of modernisation, transforming itself from a secluded, agrarian society into a centralised, industrial power in an astonishingly short period. The Meiji leaders recognised that, to survive in a world increasingly dominated by Western colonial powers, Japan needed to fundamentally alter its political, economic, and social structures. The rallying cry of this era was *fukoku kyohei*, or "enrich the country, strengthen the military," which symbolised the spirit of Meiji reforms. This guiding philosophy shaped every aspect of Japan's transformation, laying the groundwork for the nation's rapid industrialisation and eventual emergence as a formidable global force.

One of the first and most significant reforms of the Meiji government was the dissolution of the feudal domains. Under the Tokugawa shogunate, power was decentralised, with various *daimyo*, or regional lords, controlling their own territories and resources. This fragmented system, while effective in maintaining order during the Edo period, was ill-suited for a modern state. The Meiji government moved quickly to abolish the domains, consolidating power under the emperor. This centralisation enabled the creation of a unified national government, allowing Japan to pursue large-scale reforms with an efficiency that would have been impossible under the old feudal structure.

In tandem with the abolition of the domains, the Meiji government implemented sweeping land reforms. Farmers, who had previously been tied to the land through a rigid system of taxation and obligations to their lords, were given the right to own land outright. This move was revolutionary, breaking centuries-old bonds between farmers and the ruling elite, and effectively creating a new class of independent landowners. Land reform not only fostered a sense of individual ownership but also provided the government with a reliable source of revenue through a standardised land tax. This tax became a cornerstone of the new economy, funding the state's ambitious infrastructure projects and military expansion.

Education was another cornerstone of the Meiji reforms. Recognising that a modern economy required an educated workforce, the government instituted a compulsory education system that emphasised both Western science and technology and traditional Japanese values. By educating the populace in subjects like mathematics, engineering, and Western languages, Japan aimed to equip its citizens with the skills necessary to compete on the global stage. But the education system was not solely about practical skills; it also served as a vehicle for instilling loyalty to the emperor and a sense of national identity. This dual focus on technical expertise and patriotism created a workforce that was not only skilled but also deeply committed to Japan's development as a modern nation.

The reforms also extended to the military. Inspired by the Prussian and British models, the Meiji leaders modernised Japan's armed forces, replacing the samurai class with a conscripted army. This transition was both symbolic and practical. The samurai, once the backbone of Japanese military power, found their role diminished, as the government sought to build a professional army that could defend Japan against foreign threats. This shift marked the end of the samurai era, with its emphasis on feudal loyalty, and the beginning of a new era defined by loyalty to the state. The establishment of a modern military was crucial to Japan's strategic goals, as it enabled the nation to project power abroad, particularly in East Asia, where Japan would soon begin to exert its influence.

Industry and infrastructure development were also high on the Meiji agenda. The government invested heavily in building railways, telegraph lines, and modern ports, laying the foundations for a national infrastructure that would support rapid industrial growth. The Meiji leaders were acutely aware that Japan's lack of natural resources, particularly coal and iron, would hinder its development. To address this, they actively encouraged industrialisation, inviting foreign experts to Japan and sending Japanese students abroad to study Western technologies. Factories began to spring up across the country, producing textiles, steel, and other essential materials that fuelled Japan's growth. The state played a direct role in these developments, either by establishing industries outright or by supporting private entrepreneurs, creating a unique model of government-business collaboration that would become a hallmark of Japan's economy.

The rapid industrialisation of Japan had profound social consequences. The traditional social order, based on Confucian principles and a rigid hierarchy, began to erode as people moved from rural areas to cities in search of work. This migration created a new urban working class, exposed to new ideas and experiences that contrasted sharply with their rural, agrarian origins. While the government maintained a strong emphasis on social harmony and loyalty, the economic changes unleashed by industrialisation were beginning to reshape Japanese society in unexpected ways. The shift from a caste-based to a class-based society laid the groundwork for the complex social dynamics that would later define Japan's corporate culture.

Despite these dramatic changes, the Meiji government was careful to retain certain elements of traditional Japanese identity. For example, Shintoism was promoted as a national religion, reinforcing the emperor's role as a divine figure and instilling a sense of unity and continuity with Japan's past. This emphasis on cultural heritage allowed the Japanese to embrace modernity without feeling as though they were abandoning their roots. The ability to integrate Western practices with Japanese traditions became one of the defining characteristics of Meiji-era Japan and remains a cornerstone of Japanese society today.

The Meiji-era reforms transformed Japan into a nation that could compete with Western powers on equal footing. However, these changes were not universally welcomed. Many Japanese, particularly the samurai, resisted the erosion of traditional values and the rise of a Western-style economy. This tension between old and new, East and West, would continue to shape Japan's development in the decades to come. The Meiji Restoration was not just a period of modernisation; it was a profound reimagining of what it meant to be Japanese in a world dominated by Western ideals.

The legacies of these reforms are still visible in Japan's corporate and social structures. The emphasis on hierarchy, loyalty to the group, and respect for authority are all remnants of the Meiji period, adapted for a modern context. Understanding this historical foundation is crucial for foreigners who wish to navigate Japan's business culture. While Japan has certainly changed since the Meiji era, the principles that guided the nation's transformation continue to influence its approach to work, leadership, and social interactions. The Meiji Restoration was not merely a response to Western pressure; it was a calculated, deliberate strategy to preserve Japan's sovereignty and identity while embracing the tools needed to thrive in a new era.

## Social Transformation: Adopting Western Ideals and Shaping Japanese Identity

THE MEIJI RESTORATION was not only about political and economic reform but also about reshaping Japanese society to meet the demands of a modern nation. For the leaders of the Meiji era, it was clear that Japan could not rely solely on industrialisation and military strength; it also needed a societal shift towards values and practices that would align with its new status in the world. To achieve this, the Japanese government took active steps to introduce Western ideals, social norms, and cultural practices, while attempting to preserve a distinctly Japanese identity. This balancing act between tradition and modernity became a defining feature of Japanese society.

One of the most visible changes during the Meiji era was the introduction of Western-style clothing, architecture, and lifestyle choices among the upper classes. The Japanese government encouraged these adaptations to showcase Japan's willingness to modernise and participate in the global community. Government officials, businessmen, and military officers were often seen in Western suits, a radical departure from traditional attire. Western-style buildings began to replace older, wooden structures in cities, symbolising the nation's break with its feudal past. While these changes were initially met with resistance, particularly among conservative factions, they soon became status symbols, indicating progress and sophistication. For foreign observers, these visible transformations provided concrete evidence of Japan's commitment to becoming a "civilised" nation.

However, Westernisation was never about blind imitation. Japanese leaders were selective in their adoption of Western practices, carefully choosing elements they believed would benefit Japan while discarding those they deemed incompatible with Japanese values. For example, while Western science and technology were eagerly embraced, aspects of Western individualism and liberal democracy were treated with caution. Japan's leaders believed that Western individualism could undermine social harmony, a core Japanese value. Instead, they sought to instil a sense of national identity and duty that would support Japan's modernisation without eroding the country's social fabric. The government promoted the concept of *kokutai*, or "national essence," which emphasised loyalty to the emperor and the nation as a collective entity, preserving a sense of unity amidst rapid change.

Education became a crucial tool for embedding these new ideals. The Meiji government reformed Japan's education system to align with its modernisation goals, focusing not only on practical subjects like mathematics and engineering but also on fostering loyalty to the emperor and the state. A national curriculum was introduced, incorporating Western sciences and languages, which exposed students to new ways of thinking. However, the curriculum was also steeped in Japanese history, ethics, and reverence for the emperor. This dual approach created a generation of Japanese who were equipped with the knowledge and skills of the West but retained a deep sense of cultural identity. The education system was perhaps one of the most successful aspects of Japan's modernisation, as it produced a populace that could thrive in a rapidly changing world without losing sight of their heritage.

The role of women also underwent significant shifts during this period, though changes were more conservative than in other areas. The Meiji government initially promoted a vision of women as homemakers and supporters of the family unit, which was seen as essential to national stability. However, as Japan modernised, the demand for labour and the influence of Western ideals began to alter perceptions of women's roles in society. Women entered the workforce in factories and textile mills, marking the first steps towards economic independence for Japanese women. Additionally, educational reforms granted women access to basic schooling, enabling them to contribute to Japan's industrial growth. While the Meiji period did not bring about gender equality, it did lay the groundwork for future discussions on women's rights and roles within Japanese society.

Religion also underwent a transformation in the Meiji era. The government promoted Shintoism as a state religion to strengthen national identity, elevating the emperor as a divine figure and linking Shinto beliefs with patriotism. This state-sponsored version of Shintoism served as a unifying force, encouraging citizens to see their loyalty to the emperor as both a spiritual and civic duty. Buddhism, which had been influential for centuries, was suppressed to a degree, as it was seen as foreign in origin and potentially divisive. The government's efforts to establish Shintoism as a national faith were part of a broader attempt to create a homogenous cultural identity that could withstand the pressures of Westernisation.

One of the most striking aspects of Japan's social transformation during the Meiji period was the focus on fostering a collective mindset over individual expression. In the West, industrialisation often accompanied a rise in individualism, as people moved to cities and became less dependent on traditional social structures. In Japan, however, modernisation was framed as a national effort, and individual ambitions were encouraged only insofar as they contributed to the greater good. This emphasis on collective success over personal gain became embedded in Japan's corporate and social culture, with long-lasting effects that are still evident in Japanese workplaces today. The idea of *wa*, or harmony, was emphasised as essential to national progress, ensuring that societal changes did not fracture the unity of the Japanese people.

The Meiji government also took steps to reshape Japan's social hierarchy. The rigid class distinctions of the Edo period, which had placed samurai, farmers, artisans, and merchants in strict order, were dismantled. While this dismantling was initially aimed at erasing the privileges of the samurai class, it had far-reaching consequences for Japanese society as a whole. By opening up opportunities based on merit rather than birth, the government fostered a new kind of social mobility. The samurai class, once the ruling elite, was integrated into the broader society as Japan's new military and bureaucratic elite, while farmers, artisans, and merchants found new avenues for success in the emerging capitalist economy. This fluidity within the social structure allowed Japan to cultivate a diverse workforce, which was essential for its rapid industrialisation.

These social transformations were not without tension. Many Japanese were uneasy about the pace and scope of the changes, fearing that Japan was losing its cultural essence. Critics argued that Westernisation was eroding Japanese values, and they warned against adopting foreign practices without careful consideration. Writers, artists, and intellectuals voiced their concerns through literature, art, and philosophy, grappling with the question of what it meant to be Japanese in an era of unprecedented change. This tension between tradition and modernity continues to shape Japanese society, particularly in the corporate world, where Western practices have been adapted but never fully assimilated.

The Meiji period was an era of profound social transformation, during which Japan redefined itself as a modern nation while preserving a unique cultural identity. By selectively adopting Western ideals, the Meiji leaders crafted a society that could compete on the world stage without losing its sense of self. This period set the stage for the complex dynamics of Japanese corporate culture, where traditional values of hierarchy, loyalty, and harmony coexist with Western notions of efficiency and innovation. For those seeking to understand Japan's modern social landscape, the Meiji era offers essential insights into the balancing act that defines Japanese identity. The lessons learned during this period—about adapting foreign influence while retaining a core national identity—continue to resonate in Japan's approach to the globalised world today.

## The Influence of the West: Militarisation and the Emergence of Empire

AS JAPAN EMBRACED WESTERN technology and industry during the Meiji era, it also took notice of the military power wielded by Western nations. Japan's leaders recognised that in order to maintain independence, they needed not only to modernise their economy but also to develop a formidable military presence. This was not simply a matter of defence but a strategy for securing Japan's place in an increasingly competitive and imperialistic world. Japan's newfound focus on militarisation laid the groundwork for its emergence as an empire, one that would ultimately reshape East Asia and challenge Western dominance in the region.

The Japanese military reforms of the Meiji period were inspired by some of the most advanced armies in the world at that time. The Japanese government studied European military systems extensively, particularly those of Prussia and the British Navy. By implementing conscription in 1873, Japan moved away from a military composed solely of samurai and created a modern national army. The shift from a samurai-dominated force to a conscripted army was significant, not only for the military itself but for Japanese society at large. No longer would military service be confined to a hereditary warrior class; instead, all male citizens were required to serve, fostering a sense of national unity and shared purpose.

The conscription system also had a profound social impact, as it dismantled the traditional samurai class and integrated men from all walks of life into the military. The training and discipline instilled in these conscripts fostered a collective identity that transcended regional loyalties and social backgrounds. This was not merely a tactical move but a calculated effort to unify the population under a common nationalistic spirit. By breaking down class barriers within the military, the government cultivated a loyalty to the state and emperor that went beyond individual interests. This shift towards collective identity and national pride would later become a defining characteristic of Japanese society, particularly in corporate settings where loyalty to the company often parallels the loyalty once pledged to the emperor and nation.

The Western influence on Japan's military ambitions also extended to strategy and territorial expansion. In studying Western empires, Japan's leaders recognised that military strength was intrinsically linked to economic power and territorial control. Japan's first foray into imperialism came with the First Sino-Japanese War (1894–1895), where it sought to assert its influence over Korea and Taiwan. The victory over China was a significant moment for Japan, marking its arrival as a regional power capable of defeating a much larger nation. Taiwan became Japan's first colony, and this success emboldened Japan's leaders, who saw empire-building as essential to securing resources and markets for their rapidly industrialising economy.

This newfound imperial ambition was justified under the concept of *fukoku kyohei* ("enrich the country, strengthen the military"), which portrayed military expansion as a means of safeguarding Japan's economic interests. Japan's leaders framed these efforts as a way to protect East Asia from Western colonialism, positioning Japan as the leader of a pan-Asian movement. This justification had a powerful appeal, as it allowed Japan to present itself not as a coloniser in the Western sense, but as a protector of Asian sovereignty. However, Japan's imperialism ultimately mirrored many aspects of Western colonialism, as it sought to dominate its neighbours and extract resources for its own benefit.

The success of Japan's military modernisation and territorial expansion further deepened the nation's commitment to the path of empire. In 1904, Japan went to war with Russia over influence in Korea and Manchuria, a conflict that culminated in the Russo-Japanese War. Japan's victory in this war stunned the world, as it marked the first time an Asian power had defeated a European one in modern warfare. This victory had profound implications for Japan's national identity, fostering a sense of pride and superiority that solidified Japan's place as a major player on the global stage. For many Japanese, the war with Russia was proof that Japan's modernisation efforts had paid off and that it was capable of standing shoulder-to-shoulder with Western powers.

While these military successes bolstered Japan's confidence, they also laid the foundation for a more aggressive and authoritarian nationalism. Japan's government began to promote the idea of *kokutai*, a concept that emphasised loyalty to the emperor and the nation above all else. *Kokutai* became a central tenet of Japanese identity, shaping the way Japanese people viewed themselves and their relationship to the state. This ideology was not just about patriotism; it was about subjugating personal desires for the sake of the nation. *Kokutai* would later become a powerful tool for Japan's leaders to mobilise the population for war and justify aggressive policies.

In the corporate world, the militaristic and hierarchical ethos that developed during the Meiji era would later manifest in Japan's unique approach to business. Companies adopted a similar structure to the military, with clear lines of authority and an emphasis on loyalty and obedience. The idea that one should "die for the company," much like soldiers for the emperor, became a pervasive mindset in the 20th century, especially in Japan's economic boom post-WWII. The sense of duty to one's organisation mirrored the duty to one's country, a sentiment deeply rooted in the Meiji-era militarisation.

However, this militaristic approach also introduced a certain rigidity to Japanese society, as hierarchy and deference to authority became defining features of the social order. In the military, obedience was paramount, and questioning one's superior was rarely tolerated. This attitude carried over into the corporate world, where it became common for employees to follow orders without question, even at the cost of personal wellbeing. This aspect of Japanese corporate culture—deference to authority and reluctance to challenge decisions—can be traced back to the values instilled during the Meiji era, where loyalty to the state was paramount.

The legacy of Japan's militarisation during the Meiji period is complex. On one hand, it allowed Japan to protect its sovereignty, build an empire, and establish itself as a global power. On the other hand, it fostered a form of nationalism that demanded absolute loyalty, a mindset that persists in Japan's corporate culture today. For foreigners attempting to navigate Japanese workplaces, understanding this historical context is crucial. The hierarchical structure, the emphasis on loyalty, and the reluctance to question authority all stem from a militaristic ethos born in the Meiji era and solidified through Japan's imperial ambitions.

While Japan's imperialism ultimately led to devastating consequences in the 20th century, the influence of this era remains embedded in the way Japanese organisations operate. To understand Japan's corporate world is to understand a system where hierarchy, loyalty, and discipline are not just workplace norms but cultural imperatives. This militaristic structure may seem restrictive to Westerners, but for many Japanese, it represents stability and order—a legacy of Japan's determination to maintain sovereignty and identity in a world dominated by foreign powers.

## Lessons from the Post-Meiji Era: The Foundation of Japan's Modern Corporate Hierarchies

THE MEIJI RESTORATION and subsequent militarisation reshaped Japan into a nation that prided itself on efficiency, loyalty, and collective identity. However, the legacy of the Meiji reforms extended well beyond the military or imperial pursuits; it deeply influenced Japan's corporate and workplace culture. By the early 20th century, Japan's government had successfully laid the groundwork for a modern industrial economy that operated with the same rigor and hierarchy as its military. This approach to structure and discipline fostered a corporate environment that, while often admired for its efficiency, also presented challenges for individuality and adaptability. The lessons learned during Japan's post-Meiji transition became the blueprint for its corporate hierarchies, defining the roles, responsibilities, and unwritten rules that govern Japanese workplaces today.

One of the most profound impacts of the Meiji era on Japanese corporate culture is the concept of hierarchy. Just as Japan's military was organised with a strict chain of command, so too were its corporations.

The values of loyalty and respect for authority were carried over from the military into the corporate sphere, creating an environment where individuals were expected to show unwavering commitment to their superiors. This structure was not merely about maintaining order; it was a way of ensuring that each employee saw themselves as part of a larger whole, where personal ambitions were secondary to the success of the company. The term *kaisha*, or "company," became synonymous with loyalty and identity, much like the loyalty that soldiers once pledged to the emperor.

This emphasis on loyalty to the company gave rise to the notion of *lifetime employment*, a practice that became widespread in Japan by the mid-20th century. Under this system, employees were expected to remain with a single company for their entire careers, creating a bond between worker and employer that was akin to a family relationship. In return, companies offered job security, extensive benefits, and a sense of stability that became a hallmark of Japanese corporate culture. The idea was that just as a soldier's life was devoted to the nation, an employee's career was devoted to the company. This mutual loyalty reinforced the hierarchical structure, as employees were often promoted based on seniority rather than merit, preserving the status quo and ensuring that authority was respected.

However, this approach to hierarchy came with its own set of challenges. Just as questioning one's superior in the military was discouraged, so too was challenging authority within the company. Employees were expected to follow instructions without dissent, even if they believed a decision was flawed. This unspoken rule of deference created an environment where innovation and individuality were often stifled. While Western companies encouraged initiative and rewarded risk-taking, Japanese companies prioritised consensus and conformity. Decisions were typically made through a process known as *ringi-sho*, where proposals circulated from the bottom up, gathering approvals at each level. This process ensured that every voice was heard, but it also slowed decision-making, as no one wanted to disrupt harmony or appear insubordinate.

The culture of *wa*, or harmony, was crucial in this system. In Japanese society, maintaining harmony within the group is often more important than expressing one's opinions. This value has its roots in the Meiji period's emphasis on collective identity and has continued to shape Japanese corporate culture. Within a company, employees are expected to prioritise the needs of the team, often working late into the night, sacrificing personal time, and refraining from voicing strong opinions if they might cause discord. This expectation can be challenging for foreigners, who may be used to a more individualistic work environment where open debate is encouraged. In Japan, however, the goal is not to stand out but to blend in seamlessly, ensuring that the team functions as a cohesive unit.

Another legacy of the Meiji period is the *senpai-kohai* (senior-junior) relationship, a dynamic that permeates Japanese workplaces. This structure assigns respect and authority based on seniority, with younger employees expected to defer to their elders. The *senpai-kohai* relationship fosters a sense of responsibility among senior employees, who are expected to mentor and guide their juniors, much like military officers would train their subordinates. However, it also creates a rigid structure where younger employees may hesitate to offer new ideas or challenge outdated practices. This seniority-based system ensures a stable work environment but can be a barrier to flexibility and innovation. It's a double-edged sword: while it promotes stability and loyalty, it can also reinforce stagnation and reluctance to adapt to change.

The influence of the Meiji-era militaristic mindset also manifests in the concept of *gaman*, or enduring hardship without complaint. In the workplace, employees are expected to show resilience and a willingness to endure long hours, challenging projects, or demanding managers without voicing dissatisfaction. This stoicism is valued as a sign of commitment and loyalty. While Western workplaces might encourage employees to speak up about concerns for their well-being or work-life balance, Japanese companies often view such complaints as disruptive. The expectation of *gaman* can be difficult for foreigners to understand, as it sometimes leads to situations where employees experience burnout or stress-related illnesses but feel unable to seek help. The pressure to conform to this cultural norm is strong, and breaking away from it can be seen as a lack of dedication.

Moreover, Japan's approach to job roles and responsibilities is unique and can be traced back to the Meiji period's emphasis on collective identity. Unlike in many Western companies, where employees have specific, well-defined roles, Japanese companies often use a more fluid structure. Employees are expected to perform a range of tasks beyond their job description, contributing wherever they are needed. This approach fosters a strong sense of teamwork and flexibility, as everyone is expected to support the group's goals. However, it can also lead to ambiguity and confusion for foreign employees who may be accustomed to clearer role boundaries. The expectation that everyone should contribute to the collective goal, regardless of individual roles, reflects the Meiji-era value of collective identity over personal ambition.

The post-Meiji corporate hierarchy was not created solely to enforce authority but to promote stability and continuity in Japanese society. However, it has also introduced rigidity, which can make it challenging for companies to adapt quickly in a fast-changing global market. While the Japanese corporate structure has proven successful in maintaining a strong internal culture, it can sometimes hinder the flexibility required for rapid innovation. For foreign professionals entering Japanese workplaces, understanding this hierarchical foundation is essential. Knowing when to conform to these norms and when to gently challenge them can make the difference between successful integration and a frustrating experience.

The Meiji era's influence on Japan's corporate structure highlights the value that Japanese culture places on harmony, loyalty, and respect for authority. In many ways, these principles have allowed Japan to create a unique and resilient corporate landscape, one that prioritises stability over volatility and long-term success over short-term gains. Yet, these same principles can be a source of friction for those who come from cultures that value individual achievement and open communication. Recognising these deep-rooted values and approaching them with respect is the first step in navigating Japan's complex corporate hierarchies—a task that, while challenging, offers a unique perspective on what it means to work in one of the world's most distinctive business environments.

# Chapter 2: Post-WWII Japan - The American Influence and Corporate Rebirth

## The American Occupation: Restructuring Japan's Economy and Society

After Japan's surrender in 1945, the country lay in ruins. Bombed-out cities, an economy in shambles, and a humbled government faced an uncertain future. It was the American occupation, led by General Douglas MacArthur, that became the defining force behind Japan's reconstruction. For nearly seven years, from 1945 to 1952, the United States oversaw a transformation unlike any other, pulling Japan out of the ashes and setting it on a path to become one of the world's most formidable economies. But let's be clear: this wasn't just charity. The United States had strategic interests at play, too. Japan, conveniently positioned in East Asia, became a key ally in the Cold War as America looked to curb Soviet influence in the region.

The occupation was as much about reshaping Japanese society as it was about rebuilding infrastructure. MacArthur and his team of advisors—many of them corporate leaders, legal scholars, and financial experts from the United States—stepped in with the intention of rebuilding Japan in America's image, or at least close enough to make it manageable. They set out to dismantle Japan's old militaristic structures, reform its education system, and democratise its government. These changes weren't optional; they were imposed, and the Japanese government, still reeling from defeat, had little choice but to comply.

For American executives, this kind of nation-building was an experiment—a chance to apply management and organisational theories on a national scale. They came in with a blueprint, ready to introduce American-style capitalism, democratic values, and a market economy that would rely on cooperation rather than coercion. But the Japanese didn't just absorb these changes passively; they reinterpreted and repurposed them. Japan, in classic fashion, took the structures provided and shaped them into something uniquely Japanese.

One of the first major reforms was the breakup of the *zaibatsu*, the powerful industrial conglomerates that had essentially held Japan's economy in a stranglehold pre-war. These family-owned giants, like Mitsui, Mitsubishi, and Sumitomo, had intertwined themselves with the government and military, fueling Japan's war machine and monopolising entire industries. For American reformers, dismantling the *zaibatsu* was a priority. They saw these conglomerates as antithetical to free-market competition and democracy, believing that breaking them up would usher in a new era of fairness and opportunity for smaller businesses. It was the corporate equivalent of antitrust on steroids.

However, Japan's approach to corporate identity was different from America's, even then. When the Americans broke up the *zaibatsu*, they expected Japan to follow the Western model: decentralised, competitive businesses thriving independently. Instead, what emerged were the *keiretsu*—looser corporate groupings that maintained close ties, cross-shareholdings, and cooperative strategies that still resembled the pre-war conglomerates. They had the same spirit of collaboration and mutual support, though they were no longer as rigidly organised. This development is a reminder that while the Japanese embraced certain American business practices, they adapted them to fit their own cultural inclinations, particularly the tendency towards collectivism over individualism.

During this occupation period, the United States also introduced labour reforms meant to give workers more rights and protections. Trade unions were encouraged, and new labour laws were put in place to limit the power of corporate executives and to create a more democratic workplace. But, once again, these reforms didn't quite work out as the Americans had envisioned. Japanese employees weren't interested in Western-style labour movements where individual rights often came first. Instead, they embraced a model of loyalty to the company that would become the hallmark of Japanese corporate culture. Out of these reforms emerged the concept of *lifetime employment*, a model that couldn't be more different from the at-will employment common in the United States.

Imagine the reaction of an American executive stepping into this scene, expecting a new, democratised Japan only to find a workforce that viewed the company almost like a family, with loyalty to the employer as paramount. *Lifetime employment* created a bond between worker and employer that, in Japan, carried an unspoken weight. Once you joined a company, you were there for life, barring extraordinary circumstances. In return, companies provided job security and benefits, fostering a sense of stability and unity. This system was practically unheard of in the United States, where individual success and mobility were often valued over institutional loyalty. It was as if the Japanese had taken the Americans' democratic labour reforms and twisted them into a uniquely Japanese corporate ideal, one that was less about individual rights and more about collective identity.

As MacArthur and his team reshaped Japan, they also restructured its educational system to reflect democratic values. New textbooks, new curricula, and a greater focus on individual development were all part of the reforms, meant to encourage a more open-minded and free-thinking population. But Japan, yet again, adapted these changes selectively. While critical thinking was encouraged on paper, in practice, the Japanese education system retained a strong emphasis on group harmony and respect for authority. The culture of hierarchy persisted, and students were taught to find their place within the group rather than challenge it. For American educators who envisioned free-spirited classrooms, Japan's adaptation must have felt like a concession to old habits.

In the end, the American occupation laid the groundwork for Japan's economic rebirth, but the Japanese didn't simply accept American values wholesale. They rebuilt their economy on their own terms, taking what they needed from the U.S. playbook and blending it with Japan's deep-rooted traditions. The resulting corporate culture became a hybrid: part American-style capitalism, part Japanese collectivism and hierarchy. For those of us familiar with a more fluid, competitive marketplace, Japanese corporate culture might appear rigid, even perplexing at times. But it's hard not to respect the way Japan managed to take foreign influence and mould it into something that suited its own values.

From the outside, it's easy to see the influence of America in post-war Japan. The skyscrapers, the bustling financial districts, the emphasis on efficiency and productivity—all these elements speak to a modernisation influenced by Western ideals. Yet, beneath that polished exterior lies a culture that remains uniquely Japanese, a culture that values stability, loyalty, and the collective good over individual ambition. As an American corporate leader, I've seen the strengths and the limitations of both systems, and Japan's approach—while different from ours—has its own merits.

In retrospect, the occupation was a remarkable chapter in Japan's history. It was a period of profound change, led by American ideals but guided by Japanese values. The Americans came in with a plan, but Japan emerged with its own version of modernity. In this dance between East and West, Japan showed that while it could adapt, it would never simply conform. And for a country devastated by war, that resilience became the foundation of a post-war success story that astonished the world.

## Douglas MacArthur and Emperor Showa: A Symbol of Power Dynamics

FEW IMAGES CAPTURE the post-war relationship between Japan and the United States quite like that famous photograph of General Douglas MacArthur standing beside Emperor Showa (Hirohito). In it, MacArthur, tall and unceremoniously dressed in his open-collared uniform, towers over a much shorter, formally dressed Emperor. The image isn't just an interesting juxtaposition of height or style—it's a visual representation of the power dynamics between the two nations in that moment. For many Americans, it symbolised victory and authority. For the Japanese, it was a bitter reminder of their defeat, but also a clear demonstration of where the new power lay.

MacArthur, known for his larger-than-life personality, wasn't just any commander. He saw himself as the man responsible for rebuilding Japan, a task he approached with all the drama of a Shakespearean hero. He liked to remind both the Japanese and his own staff that he held absolute authority. In those early post-war years, he was, in every sense, the ruler of Japan—a foreign shogun with powers granted directly by the Allies. And the Emperor? For the first time in Japanese history, his position was profoundly diminished. MacArthur's presence overshadowed him, and that famous photograph captured this change in status as succinctly as any piece of diplomacy ever could.

MacArthur was deliberate in his public appearances with the Emperor. He wanted to show the Japanese people that their leader was no longer untouchable, no longer the divine figure they had worshipped for centuries. The old system, with its rigid hierarchies and near-mythical reverence for the Emperor, was a barrier to the kind of democratic reforms MacArthur and his team wanted to implement. By putting the Emperor quite literally in his shadow, MacArthur aimed to drive home the point that the Emperor was now answerable to the Allied powers.

For the Japanese, this was a difficult pill to swallow. Emperor Showa had been a central figure in Japan's militaristic ambitions; he was, after all, the symbolic head of the state during the war. But MacArthur recognised that Showa could also be a tool for rebuilding. Rather than deposing him, which might have caused chaos, he allowed the Emperor to remain a figurehead, one who could guide the people through the transition. This choice wasn't made out of sentimentality but out of pragmatism. MacArthur understood that the Japanese people, who held deep cultural attachments to the Emperor, would be more likely to accept the sweeping reforms if they saw their monarch adjusting and moving forward with the times.

The relationship between MacArthur and Showa was a balancing act. MacArthur needed Showa to legitimise the occupation, while Showa needed MacArthur's support to retain even a symbolic role. They both understood the value of optics, and each had to tread carefully, maintaining the illusion of cooperation despite the profound shift in power. One could say it was a performance, a delicate game of public perception played out on the world stage. Both men, in their own way, represented their countries' ideals, with MacArthur embodying American dominance and Showa the enduring symbol of Japan's spirit, now tempered by humility.

This shift in power wasn't lost on the Japanese people. Many looked at that photograph and saw a direct message: the Emperor, once untouchable, was now subject to foreign authority. Yet, for all the humiliation that might have been felt, there was also a sense of relief. With Showa's role diminished, Japan was no longer bound by the extreme militaristic ambitions that had defined the pre-war era. The old ideologies of conquest and expansion had, in many ways, collapsed with the Emperor's former power. The Japanese could now focus on recovery, on rebuilding a nation that had lost much of its infrastructure and economy in the war. MacArthur's management of this transition provided the framework within which Japan would evolve.

What's remarkable is how the Japanese responded to this new order. Instead of rallying against the Americans, as some might have expected, they accepted their new circumstances with a characteristic pragmatism. This wasn't out of sheer submission or defeatism but rather an understanding that change was necessary. The Japanese people saw in the Emperor's diminished role a symbol of new beginnings, a chance to redefine their identity under a system that would bring stability and, eventually, prosperity. In a sense, MacArthur's overt show of dominance enabled the Japanese to channel their energies into constructive, rather than destructive, pathways.

For an American corporate leader observing this dynamic, there's a lesson here. Power, when wielded overtly, can create submission, but it can also open up avenues for collaboration and adaptation. MacArthur's dominance didn't completely alienate the Japanese; instead, it set boundaries within which they could operate, adapt, and eventually thrive. By accepting the change in power dynamics, the Japanese people could focus on what mattered most—rebuilding a devastated nation. As much as MacArthur's towering presence overshadowed the Emperor, it also gave Japan a clear direction in uncertain times.

This image of MacArthur and Showa is more than just a relic of history; it's a reminder of how power, presented in stark and unambiguous terms, can set the stage for transformation. It's no surprise, then, that modern Japanese corporate culture still bears traces of this interaction. Japanese companies, like their government during the occupation, have learned to balance foreign influence with cultural integrity, adopting aspects of Western management while preserving a core that remains distinctly Japanese. Much like Showa beneath

MacArthur's shadow, Japan's corporate world has learned to adapt without losing its essence.

In the years following the occupation, Japan rose from the ashes not by emulating America in every respect but by finding its own rhythm within the structures imposed by the West. They learned to accept the frameworks given to them while bending them to fit their own values. This unique approach to balance is something that Western corporate leaders, myself included, often find impressive. Japan took what it needed from us but held on to its own identity, showing a resilience and adaptability that few could have predicted in those early days of the occupation.

Ultimately, that photograph of MacArthur and Showa captures not just a moment in time, but the essence of Japan's post-war transformation: a willingness to submit when necessary, but always with a mind towards self-preservation and eventual independence. It's a symbol of humility forced by circumstance, but it's also a testament to the Japanese ability to endure, adapt, and, when the time is right, redefine themselves on their own terms.

## Post-War Economic Miracle: Rebuilding Japan's Industry with American Support

BY THE 1950S, JAPAN'S landscape had shifted from rubble and defeat to an economy on the brink of a remarkable resurgence. This transformation wasn't by chance. The Americans, with MacArthur leading the charge, had laid the groundwork to steer Japan from a war-torn state into a budding capitalist powerhouse. And as the Cold War gained momentum, Japan's economic stability became more than a matter of economic recovery—it became a linchpin in America's broader strategy to counter communism in East Asia. With American guidance and support, Japan launched into what would become known as the "post-war economic miracle."

This "miracle" was hardly an overnight success story. Rather, it was a carefully orchestrated mix of American investment, industrial restructuring, and a Japanese workforce willing to endure grueling hours for the sake of national pride. The United States poured in capital and resources, initially to stabilise Japan but ultimately to create a stronghold in the East that would counterbalance communist China and the Soviet Union. As far as American corporate interests were concerned, Japan was a blank slate, ripe for Western-style capitalism, albeit in a form that ended up looking distinctly Japanese.

The Americans first focused on rebuilding Japan's industrial capacity. Japan's industries had been heavily bombed during the war, leaving little infrastructure in place. Recognising the strategic importance of Japan as an industrial hub, the U.S. government, along with American corporations, provided technology, funding, and even training to Japanese companies. The keiretsu structure—those interconnected business groups that had evolved from the pre-war *zaibatsu*—became a major focal point. These conglomerates, which included the likes of Mitsubishi, Sumitomo, and Mitsui, had previously been dismantled during the occupation. But by the 1950s, they were back, operating with a new form of structure that allowed Japan's corporations to rebuild collectively, pooling resources and sharing technological advancements without formally merging.

In many ways, Japan's post-war corporate revival was a unique blend of American-style capitalism and Japanese collectivism. Unlike American companies, which thrived on competition and profit-driven goals, Japanese firms placed a premium on group cohesion and stability. This approach, at first glance, seemed almost anti-capitalistic to American observers. But the strategy was clear to the Japanese: stability would lead to steady growth, and in turn, to prosperity for all. American corporations and economists watched with a mix of admiration and confusion. Here was a nation adopting capitalism, yet refusing to embrace its more individualistic, competitive components.

It was an approach that seemed contradictory, but it would prove to be exceptionally effective.

I remember reading about how Japan's manufacturers, like Sony and Toyota, began by making inexpensive consumer goods, which were initially dismissed by Western competitors as cheap knock-offs. American executives saw these early Japanese products—radios, cameras, and motorcycles—and thought, "There's no way this is going to compete with our quality." But the Japanese had a different strategy in mind. They focused on constant improvement, known in Japan as *kaizen*, the practice of continuous, incremental improvement. By the 1960s, Japanese goods were no longer considered inferior; in fact, they were starting to dominate global markets, from automobiles to electronics.

The Americans contributed to Japan's transformation not only with investments but by facilitating access to new technologies and global markets. American corporations partnered with Japanese firms, sharing production methods and quality control standards. This partnership led to significant advancements in manufacturing, and Japanese companies rapidly adopted practices like assembly-line efficiency and standardisation. But again, they didn't simply copy these techniques—they refined them. Where American factories focused on output, Japanese factories focused on minimising waste, enhancing efficiency, and ensuring that every part met stringent quality standards.

This commitment to quality was more than just a corporate goal; it became a national ethos. I've heard anecdotes about Japanese workers who took such pride in their work that they'd willingly stay late to fix any issues, unpaid, before a product hit the shelves. In America, this level of dedication would be unusual, if not unheard of—our culture values hard work, sure, but we also know where to draw the line. Japan's workforce, on the other hand, was fueled by a sense of collective responsibility that came to define its post-war economic model.

The relationship between the Japanese government and its corporations was another key factor in the economic miracle. Unlike the relatively hands-off approach in the United States, where corporations operate independently, Japan's Ministry of International Trade and Industry (MITI) took an active role in guiding corporate growth. MITI essentially acted as a silent partner, setting industrial priorities, coordinating resource allocation, and even suggesting pricing strategies. This kind of government-corporate partnership was almost unthinkable in the United States, where we prize a free market. But in Japan, it worked seamlessly. The government wasn't seen as a regulator in the American sense; it was a supporter, a strategic partner working alongside corporations to build the nation's future.

One aspect of this era that fascinated me was the emergence of the *salaryman*—the committed, often overworked employee who dedicated his life to his company. In the United States, we'd call someone like this a "company man," but there's a difference. The American company man might be devoted to his job, sure, but he's also got one eye on his personal aspirations, his family life, maybe even a side business. The Japanese *salaryman*, on the other hand, was expected to live and breathe for the company, sacrificing his personal life for corporate success. This level of devotion was almost shocking to American observers, who saw it as borderline excessive. Yet, it became a cornerstone of Japan's corporate identity, driving the workforce to put in longer hours and stay with a single employer for life.

By the 1970s, Japan's economic miracle was in full swing. Industries like steel, automobiles, and electronics were booming, and Japan was exporting high-quality products worldwide. American business leaders began to notice, and not without a touch of alarm, that Japan was quickly catching up in fields where the U.S. had once held unchallenged dominance. The Japanese had taken American techniques, refined them with their own methods, and created a powerful economic machine that was now competing directly with the West. Some

American companies tried to adopt Japanese practices, like *kaizen* and just-in-time manufacturing, but without the same level of cultural cohesion, the results were mixed. What worked for Japan, rooted in their collective mindset and emphasis on harmony, didn't always translate neatly to the more individualistic, profit-driven environment in the States.

The Japanese economic miracle wasn't about blind adoption of Western practices. It was about adaptation—taking what worked, discarding what didn't, and maintaining a cultural core that prioritised stability and collective success. The United States had provided the tools, the financing, and even some of the business strategies, but the Japanese had applied them with a distinctly Japanese touch. This approach wasn't simply a response to foreign occupation; it was a calculated, culturally ingrained process that turned Japan into a global economic powerhouse.

In looking at Japan's post-war economic rise, there's a lesson for any corporate leader willing to see it. Japan didn't succeed by copying the American model outright. They succeeded by knowing exactly what to take and what to leave behind, shaping their own path based on cultural values that have been honed over centuries. As an American, I might sometimes raise an eyebrow at Japan's "all-in" work culture or the almost familial loyalty shown to employers, but I can't argue with the results. Japan's economic miracle showed the world that rebuilding isn't just about resources—it's about resilience, adaptability, and an unwavering sense of purpose.

## The Rise of Lifetime Employment: Security Over Innovation

BY THE TIME JAPAN'S economy was booming in the 1960s, one of the most defining features of its corporate landscape was in place: *lifetime employment*. For many outside Japan, this concept seemed almost anachronistic, even outlandish—a model where a company effectively becomes a lifelong partner, promising job security in exchange for unwavering loyalty. For Americans used to the flexibility of the job market, where promotions often mean switching companies or even industries, Japan's *lifetime employment* system looked rigid, a relic in an era where adaptability seemed to be the new currency. But the Japanese weren't aiming to follow global trends—they were cultivating something entirely their own.

This system of lifetime employment was born out of necessity. After World War II, with much of Japan's industry in tatters and the nation desperate to rebuild, stability was the primary concern. Companies needed a dedicated workforce that wouldn't jump ship, and employees, in turn, sought assurance that they wouldn't be cast aside if the economy took another downturn. The government backed this structure, encouraging companies to provide secure, long-term employment as a way to stabilise Japanese society. So, from a practical standpoint, lifetime employment was a kind of social contract: companies would take care of their employees, and in return, employees would remain loyal, effectively tying their personal identities to the company.

In American terms, the concept of job loyalty isn't alien, but it's also not foundational. We prize the "self-made man," the ability to pivot, to climb the ladder by moving up and out. In Japan, however, career mobility was almost unheard of within this framework. Once you joined a company, the expectation was that you'd stay until retirement, climbing the ranks through seniority rather than ambition. And this wasn't just about loyalty—it was about *wa*, the emphasis on group harmony that runs deep in Japanese culture. For the Japanese, a stable career within a single company wasn't just a job; it was a way to maintain societal stability, a place where they could devote themselves without distraction.

I remember my first experience with this when I sat in on a meeting at a major Japanese manufacturing firm. I noticed that most of the employees were of a similar age, the same faces one might have seen there 20 years prior. They talked about the company with a kind of reverence I hadn't seen much back home. In the U.S., when someone says, "I've been here for 20 years," it's often accompanied by a sigh or even a sense of entrapment. But in Japan, the tone was different. There was a sense of pride in that longevity, a feeling that one's life was dedicated to the success of something larger. They weren't just employees; they were family, bound to the company as if by blood.

Of course, there's a trade-off to this security. Lifetime employment does foster loyalty and a deep-seated commitment to the company's success, but it also creates rigidity. Promotions are often based on seniority, not necessarily merit, and while this creates a sense of fairness, it can stifle innovation. I watched as younger employees kept their heads down, rarely speaking up in meetings or proposing new ideas. Why? Because they knew that without the years behind them, their voices would carry little weight. Contrast that with an American office, where the newest hire might be the first to throw out a bold idea. In Japan, hierarchy reigns, and speaking out of turn is discouraged. The system values experience over fresh perspectives, which can be a double-edged sword.

I once spoke with a Japanese manager about this, and he shrugged, saying, "Why rush? I will have time to show my ideas." He was in his thirties, content to wait until his fifties to have any real influence. For me, that was a revelation. In the States, we're used to the idea of "earning your stripes," but we also expect people to rise based on ability, not merely age. Here in Japan, however, patience is a virtue, and the waiting game is part of the process. Promotions are gradual, carefully paced, almost ceremonial. To a foreigner, it might seem like a slow-moving machine, but for the Japanese, this system ensures that leadership is stable, informed by years of accumulated knowledge and experience.

Another notable outcome of lifetime employment is the *salaryman* culture. The "company man" image is nowhere more pronounced than in Japan. The salaryman doesn't just clock in and out; he embodies the company's ethos, sacrificing personal time and even family life in favour of the company's success. This level of devotion can seem excessive to outsiders, even bordering on self-sacrifice. I've seen it firsthand: employees working late into the night, missing family dinners, all because their peers were doing the same. It's a culture where leaving on time isn't an option; it's a sign that you're not fully committed.

Yet, this dedication comes with an unwritten guarantee. As long as you uphold your end of the bargain, your job is safe. Economic downturns, company crises—these are challenges that Western companies often respond to with layoffs. In Japan, however, companies are far more reluctant to let employees go. It's a matter of honour, of responsibility. The company has taken care of you, so you are expected to weather the storm together. During the 1990s recession, for instance, Japanese firms kept employees on payroll, reducing hours or reallocating tasks rather than resorting to mass layoffs. For a Japanese worker, this commitment to job security reinforces a sense of trust, even a sense of indebtedness, to the company.

But make no mistake: there's a cost to this stability. When the company becomes a second family, individual aspirations often take a back seat. Ambitious employees looking to climb the ladder quickly find themselves at odds with the system. In a country where harmony and consensus are valued, pushing for rapid advancement can come across as selfish or even disruptive. This is not a culture that encourages mavericks or disruptors; it encourages continuity and respect for those who came before. The result is a workforce that's extraordinarily loyal but often slow to innovate. And for American executives trying to introduce change, this can be a real challenge.

For a foreigner, the lifetime employment model can be baffling. Why would anyone tie themselves to a single company for life? Why wouldn't they seek out new opportunities, higher salaries, more challenging roles? But in Japan, it's less about personal ambition and more about collective stability. The Japanese understand that, in a society as tightly woven as theirs, harmony is paramount, and the individual is, to some extent, secondary to the group. This mindset makes lifetime employment not just an economic structure, but a cultural one, a way of life that binds individuals to something greater than themselves.

As Japan's economy globalises, lifetime employment is gradually evolving, but it's not going away entirely. Younger generations are beginning to seek more mobility, and foreign firms operating in Japan are introducing new models of career advancement. But even as Japan adapts, the spirit of *lifetime employment* remains influential. It's a system that values loyalty, patience, and stability over ambition, a concept that might seem antiquated to some but still holds powerful appeal in Japan's corporate world. For an outsider, understanding this aspect of Japanese work culture is essential. It's not about productivity alone—it's about legacy, continuity, and, above all, the unwavering trust between employee and employer that, once formed, is rarely broken.

## Western Management Meets Japanese Culture: Conflicting Ideals

AS THE 1970S ROLLED into the 1980s, Japan's economic trajectory was soaring. The country had clawed its way up from post-war devastation to become a formidable force, capturing global market share in industries like electronics and automotive manufacturing. This wasn't just a recovery—it was a resurgence that positioned Japan as an economic giant, right up there with the United States. American executives started looking at Japan less like a protégé and more like a competitor, and the relationship between the two nations grew complex, teetering between admiration and rivalry.

The Japanese economic model, heavily influenced by American support post-WWII, had evolved into something distinctly Japanese. While Japan took the foundations laid by the U.S. and built an economic machine, their approach to management and corporate culture diverged sharply from the Western model. I once had a colleague remark that Japan's success was thanks to U.S. intervention, to which I'd say, "Absolutely, we helped Japan get back on its feet, but they went and made it work their own way." The Japanese had perfected practices like *kaizen* (continuous improvement) and *just-in-time* inventory, creating efficiencies that were unmatched and soon surpassed American competitors.

However, American corporate leaders found the Japanese style of management to be unconventional, even puzzling. U.S. management techniques favoured direct communication, fast-paced decision-making, and clear, merit-based career progression. Japan, on the other hand, leaned into a model grounded in hierarchy, consensus-building, and a collective approach that prized harmony above all. The infamous *ringi-sho* process, where proposals must be approved by multiple layers of hierarchy, often frustrated American executives. It felt too slow, too cautious, and, frankly, at odds with the bottom-line-driven ethos of American business.

I remember a time when an American consultant friend of mine tried to implement Western-style performance reviews in a Japanese firm. "It's about results, not rank!" he insisted, thinking he could get the employees to focus on outcomes over seniority. The attempt didn't go over well. The employees, accustomed to promotion by tenure and loyalty, balked at the idea of a merit-only review system. The consultant was baffled, but I laughed. Japanese management, for all its faults, wasn't something you could just bulldoze with American corporate ideology. Japan had its own rhythm, and trying to impose Western methods without understanding the cultural bedrock was a recipe for failure.

But as Japan's economy surged, an interesting shift occurred. The U.S. watched as Japan's GDP climbed steadily, inching closer and closer to America's. By the mid-1980s, Japan had effectively become the world's second-largest economy, and in some industries, it was outright outperforming American competitors. That's when I heard an amusing conspiracy theory from a Japanese friend: he swore that the U.S. had deliberately sabotaged Japan's economy when it got too close to surpassing America. I laughed it off, of course. From my perspective, it's perfectly logical for a sovereign country to protect its interests. If Japan was good enough, they'd outmaneuver us, right? This isn't a game for the faint of heart; it's international business, and every country plays to win.

The reality, however, was that the U.S. did take action to rein in Japan's economic momentum, particularly through the Plaza Accord of 1985. The agreement, signed between the U.S., Japan, and a few other major economies, aimed to depreciate the U.S. dollar and effectively make Japanese goods more expensive on the global market. The Accord was designed to address trade imbalances, and while it didn't explicitly target Japan, it certainly put a dent in Japan's export-driven economy. Japanese firms suddenly found themselves at a disadvantage, with the yen appreciating so quickly that many companies were priced out of key markets.

In hindsight, the Plaza Accord is often viewed as a turning point in Japan's economy—a moment when American influence shaped Japan's trajectory more overtly. To many Japanese, it felt like the U.S. was pulling the rug out from under them just as they were hitting their stride. To American leaders, it was simply sound economic strategy. After all, the U.S. had extended a hand after WWII, providing the means for Japan to rebuild. If Japan's rise was starting to put America's interests at risk, why wouldn't the U.S. act? That's the nature of the game.

The Plaza Accord and its effects, though not openly discussed in Japanese business circles, are still felt in Japan's corporate culture today. The forced yen appreciation put intense pressure on Japanese companies, prompting them to reconsider their export-heavy strategies. Many shifted production overseas, a move that altered Japan's once-insulated corporate landscape. While Japan had prided itself on a self-sufficient workforce and domestic manufacturing, companies like Sony and Toyota began setting up factories abroad to counterbalance the high costs of operating solely in Japan. This pivot would shape Japan's economy and workforce for decades, redefining "Japan Inc." on a global stage.

For the Americans who had been watching, the Plaza Accord felt like a corrective measure, a strategic move to level the playing field. For the Japanese, it was a jolt, a reminder that while they had autonomy, they were still vulnerable to external pressures. Some even see it as a wake-up call, a moment when Japan realised that simply following its unique path wasn't enough. In a way, it highlighted the tension between Japan's insular, harmonious corporate culture and the cutthroat realities of the global economy. They were reminded, painfully, that America might have been their post-war "saviour," but it was also their fiercest competitor.

In the aftermath, Japan's corporate leaders adopted a more cautious stance. Many companies doubled down on the values of loyalty and stability, but the pressure to adapt to global competition meant that cracks were beginning to show in the lifetime employment system and hierarchical structures. For Japanese corporations, the challenge was clear: could they maintain their identity in a world increasingly driven by Western-style capitalism, or would they have to adopt a more flexible approach?

Reflecting on these events, I can't help but see the Plaza Accord as a necessary reminder that, in business, allies today may be rivals tomorrow. Japan's unique blend of cultural tradition and corporate resilience had taken it far, but global economics waits for no one. They had to recalibrate, adjust, and come to terms with the fact that the game isn't fair and doesn't reward second place.

Ultimately, the Plaza Accord stands as a lesson in economic realpolitik. Japan may have taken a hit, but they didn't fold. They adapted, albeit slowly, recalibrating their strategies and proving that even under external pressures, they could weather the storm. For American executives, the episode was a testament to the value of leverage. For Japan, it was a reminder that the world stage is no place for complacency. You either keep up or get left behind.

## Japan Inc.: The Birth of Japan's Unique Corporate Identity

BY THE LATE 1980S, Japan had become synonymous with economic power and industrial prowess. Its corporations were not only expanding globally but were also solidifying their place as benchmarks in efficiency, quality, and innovation. Terms like "Japan Inc." began circulating in business circles, a nickname that hinted at the unusual blend of corporate identity and national pride that characterised Japanese businesses. Unlike in the U.S., where companies are seen as independent entities that happen to be headquartered in America, Japanese corporations operated almost as if they were arms of the state—united in their goal to elevate Japan on the world stage. This alignment between corporate and national identity gave Japan a distinctive advantage, but it also presented challenges that would come to define "Japan Inc."

The phrase "Japan Inc." speaks to the near-symbiotic relationship between the Japanese government and its largest corporations, a relationship that has its roots in the post-war reconstruction period. During those crucial years of rebuilding, the Japanese government took a hands-on approach, guiding industrial growth through policies, subsidies, and close coordination with leading companies. This wasn't a typical free-market setup; it was a strategy, almost like a corporate-national partnership. The Ministry of International Trade and Industry (MITI) became a powerful force, not merely regulating industry but actively shaping it. They identified key sectors—automobiles, electronics, and steel, for example—as strategic industries, providing them with resources and support to ensure they would dominate globally.

To an American executive, this level of state involvement in corporate affairs would have seemed excessive, even meddlesome. In the U.S., the government regulates but rarely intervenes to this extent. We prefer a marketplace where the best company wins, based on its own merits. But the Japanese approach was different—they viewed their industries almost as a collective force, with individual companies working not just for profit but for the prestige and growth of Japan as a whole. And, for a time, this strategy was staggeringly effective. By pooling resources, sharing knowledge, and setting common goals, Japanese firms could innovate faster, enter markets more competitively, and outperform rivals from countries where the government kept its distance.

What's remarkable is how deeply this national mission affected the mindset of Japanese employees. Working for a major Japanese corporation wasn't just a job; it was a duty, almost an honour. Many employees saw themselves as representatives of Japan's future, dedicating their careers to the company with a sense of loyalty that felt foreign, almost excessive, to Western observers. I once had a Japanese colleague tell me, "In America, you work for yourself; in Japan, we work for our country." There was a pride in his voice that I couldn't ignore. American workers might feel patriotic about their nation, but few would ever tie that sentiment directly to their company.

For Japanese companies, this loyalty and sense of purpose fostered an almost military-like discipline and coordination. At its peak, "Japan Inc." functioned as a well-oiled machine, where each company, large or small, felt its work was part of a greater national endeavour. It was a culture of synergy, where rivalries were subdued in favour of shared success. Companies routinely worked together, sharing technologies, supply chains, and even personnel when it served a greater purpose. In Japan, competition was internal, a drive to perfect their own systems and products rather than to undercut a fellow Japanese firm. In the U.S., where competition between companies—sometimes even between departments—is encouraged, this collaborative mindset felt almost radical.

But this unity also came with limitations. The cooperative, harmony-driven structure meant that change was slow and often met with resistance. With everyone working in unison, questioning the status quo became risky. I recall a conversation with a Japanese executive who admitted, "We move carefully because we have to make sure everyone is comfortable. We don't want to disrupt things too quickly." In Japan, innovation came through refinement rather than disruption, through steady improvement rather than risky leaps. It was this meticulous approach that made Japanese products so reliable, but it also meant that "Japan Inc." could sometimes be slow to react to rapid shifts in the market.

As Japan's economy grew, so did its sense of self-assurance. Japanese corporations began buying up iconic American assets in the 1980s—movie studios, real estate, even golf courses. This purchasing spree made headlines, and not all of them flattering. In the States, people began to talk about Japanese companies as if they were quietly taking over, raising questions about Japan's intentions and stirring a bit of public unease. I remember seeing headlines at the time that painted Japanese companies as almost predatory. To Americans, it felt as though Japan, having benefitted from U.S. support post-war, was now encroaching on American economic turf.

But this view, I'd argue, misses the point. Japan wasn't out to take over; they were proving themselves on the world stage, driven by the belief that their companies' successes would elevate Japan's global standing. The purchases weren't acts of hostility—they were declarations of economic capability. When a Japanese company bought Rockefeller Center, it was a signal that Japan had arrived. They wanted a seat at the table, and they weren't content with just a peripheral view. For an American, the idea of buying foreign assets out of national pride might seem odd, but for Japan Inc., it made perfect sense. It was both business and symbolic victory.

Yet, for all its strengths, the "Japan Inc." model showed its limitations when the bubble economy burst in the early 1990s. Suddenly, the very attributes that had propelled Japan to the top—its harmony, collective identity, and government-corporate partnership—became barriers to recovery. Companies that had been so closely tied to the state found it hard to adapt to a downturn. The keiretsu structure, which encouraged internal cohesion, struggled to adjust as the economy contracted. Companies were reluctant to downsize or adapt aggressively, hoping that the government or MITI would step in to stabilise things, as it had in the past. The lack of flexibility, once seen as a strength, now became a hindrance.

In the years following the bubble, Japan Inc. had to reckon with its own rigidity. They were no longer just competing with the U.S.; new global players like South Korea and China were emerging, adopting and sometimes outpacing Japan's strategies. The close-knit, highly coordinated approach that had once made Japan untouchable was becoming outdated. But even in the face of these challenges, Japanese corporations maintained a level of loyalty and commitment that's rare anywhere else in the world. They took their hits, but they didn't collapse.

Looking back, the idea of "Japan Inc." is a testament to what can be achieved when a nation's companies align themselves with a shared vision. The U.S. may have been Japan's economic "saviour" in the aftermath of WWII, but Japan took that foundation and built something unique. They created a corporate identity that balanced pride with humility, ambition with caution. And while the cracks in the model were revealed in the 1990s, Japan Inc. still stands as an example of the power of collective purpose. They may have borrowed from the West, but they crafted a corporate ethos that remains entirely Japanese.

For those of us accustomed to a more individualistic approach, Japan's way of doing business might seem restrictive, even suffocating. But there's something undeniably admirable about a culture that ties corporate success to national pride. Japan Inc. wasn't just about making profits; it was about proving that Japan could stand tall on the world stage. And if that meant adapting a bit of Western capitalism while still staying true to their own principles, so be it. They didn't just follow the leader—they created their own path, one that, for better or worse, still influences Japanese corporate identity today.

## The Plaza Accord and American Influence on Japan's Economy

IN 1985, A SIGNIFICANT event took place that would shape the Japanese economy for decades to come: the signing of the Plaza Accord. For those of us in the corporate world, the Accord represented a strategic move by the United States to address a growing trade imbalance, particularly with Japan. At the time, Japan's export-driven economy was booming, and the yen was undervalued relative to the dollar, which made Japanese goods cheaper and more competitive abroad. American companies were feeling the heat, with Japanese cars, electronics, and other manufactured goods dominating markets that American firms had once considered their own. From Washington's perspective, it was time for a corrective measure.

The Plaza Accord was a multi-nation agreement between the United States, Japan, West Germany, France, and the United Kingdom, aimed at depreciating the U.S. dollar relative to the yen and other currencies. For Japan, the immediate effect was that their exports would become more expensive, potentially slowing the relentless growth of their industrial sector. I remember hearing American business leaders speak with a certain pride about the Accord—it was, after all, a demonstration of U.S. economic influence on the global stage. Some saw it as a "saviour" moment for the American economy, a way to level the playing field and curb Japan's rapid ascent. But for Japan, it was a jolt that set off a chain of economic consequences.

The yen's appreciation hit Japanese exporters hard, especially companies like Toyota and Sony, which had built their success on affordable, high-quality goods. Suddenly, they were forced to reconsider their entire strategy. To offset the rising costs of exporting from Japan, many Japanese firms began to shift production overseas, setting up factories in the United States, Southeast Asia, and elsewhere. This move was pragmatic, but it also marked a shift in the Japanese approach to business. Companies that had prided themselves on being "made in Japan" now had to adapt to a global supply chain. It was a difficult transition, and one that didn't sit easily with Japanese corporate leaders who had built their reputations on domestic production.

For Japan, the Plaza Accord is often seen as a moment when American interests openly collided with their own. Some Japanese business leaders felt betrayed, as if the U.S., which had helped them rebuild after the war, was now pulling the rug out from under them just as they were achieving real global success. I even had a Japanese friend who believed, half-jokingly, that the U.S. had orchestrated the whole thing to sabotage Japan's economy. "They didn't like that we were getting too close to their GDP," he said with a smirk. I couldn't help but laugh it off. From my perspective, it's perfectly reasonable for a country to protect its own interests. If Japan's corporations were sharp enough, they would have found a way to counter the effects. After all, no one hands out advantages on a silver platter in this game.

But the impact of the Plaza Accord wasn't something Japan could just shrug off. In response to the rapid yen appreciation, Japan's central bank lowered interest rates to stimulate the economy. This flood of cheap money fueled a domestic spending spree, leading to what's now known as the bubble economy. Property values and stock prices skyrocketed, creating a financial bubble that, in hindsight, was destined to burst. The Plaza Accord may have been the catalyst, but it was Japan's reaction—the drive to maintain growth at any cost—that led to the bubble.

By the end of the 1980s, Japan was riding high on unprecedented levels of wealth. Real estate in Tokyo was so overvalued that at one point, the land beneath the Imperial Palace was said to be worth more than all of California. People and companies borrowed aggressively, confident that the value of their assets would only go up. But as we know in business, unchecked optimism is often a precursor to collapse. When the bubble finally burst in the early 1990s, it was devastating. Japan was left grappling with a recession that would last over a decade, resulting in what's now referred to as the "Lost Decade."

The Plaza Accord's legacy is a mixed one. On one hand, it temporarily alleviated the U.S. trade deficit and reined in Japan's booming export economy. But on the other hand, it set in motion economic shifts that would deeply impact Japan. The bubble's collapse revealed the vulnerabilities of Japan's highly coordinated, risk-averse corporate system. Companies that had once been the pride of "Japan Inc." struggled to adapt, weighed down by debt and declining domestic demand. Many were forced to restructure, and the age-old promise of lifetime employment came under pressure. For American executives, watching this unfold was a study in economic resilience—and sometimes, lack thereof.

Looking back, it's clear that the Plaza Accord was a strategic move on America's part. The U.S. had extended a helping hand to Japan post-WWII, fostering its growth, but when that growth threatened American economic interests, the U.S. acted decisively. For some in Japan, this felt like a betrayal, but for Americans, it was simply sound economic policy. As an American corporate leader, I can't help but see the Accord as an example of how international relations—and business, by extension—work. No one's here to hold anyone else's hand. Countries will always protect their interests, and if Japan's corporations wanted to keep up, they had to adapt.

For Japan, the Accord was a wake-up call. They had experienced the heights of economic success and then witnessed how quickly things could unravel. Japanese firms learned the hard way that dependence on a single growth model, particularly one tied to export-driven manufacturing, was risky. This realisation led to a slow but steady shift in Japanese corporate culture, one that valued diversification, globalisation, and, eventually, more flexible employment practices.

Today, Japan is no longer the economic juggernaut it once was, but the legacy of the Plaza Accord still lingers. Japanese companies are more cautious, their leaders more aware of the risks of overextension. And while Japan's corporate culture remains distinct, it has adapted to incorporate a greater understanding of global markets, competitiveness, and the need to balance national pride with practical, international considerations.

In the end, the Plaza Accord stands as a lesson in economic pragmatism. The U.S. acted to protect its interests, and Japan was forced to adjust. For all the talk of "sabotage" or betrayal, the reality is simpler: each nation was playing its hand, as any savvy player would.

Japan may have taken a hit, but they didn't crumble. Instead, they adapted, recalibrated, and continued to build on the resilience that had brought them back from post-war devastation in the first place.

# Part 2: The Structure and Dynamics of Japanese Workplace Culture

# Chapter 3: Understanding the Senpai-Kouhai Hierarchy in Workplaces

## Origins and Significance of Senpai-Kouhai

One of the most striking aspects of the *senpai-kouhai* system is the way deference is baked into daily life. A *kouhai*'s role isn't just to do their job well but to support and respect their *senpai*. This can mean something as simple as letting a *senpai* speak first in a meeting or as complex as carefully navigating around a senior's opinion, even if it's wrong. In a Western setting, we'd probably have a quick debate, throw around ideas, and eventually zero in on the best solution, but in Japan, it's different. Here, pushing your own agenda too hard isn't just seen as aggressive—it's disruptive.

Once, early in my tenure in Japan, I thought I'd make a great impression by taking the initiative in a meeting. I was met with silence—an uncomfortable silence that I quickly learned was not a show of respect but a sign that I'd overstepped. It wasn't that my ideas were unwelcome; it was that my approach was too bold, too fast for a system that values subtlety and consensus over direct confrontation. My *senpai* took me aside afterward, and in the most polite way possible, advised me to "observe a bit longer." It was a lesson in humility, a reminder that sometimes holding back can earn more respect than leading the charge.

This deference isn't blind obedience, though. The *senpai* in these relationships are expected to act as mentors, supporting their *kouhai* with guidance rather than dominance. In return, the *kouhai* isn't a passive follower but a careful observer, learning from the senior's example while waiting for the right time to share their own perspective. It's a slow dance, a quiet back-and-forth that's about timing as much as it is about respect.

For a foreigner, the trick is learning to defer without feeling diminished. You're not here to overthrow the system but to work within it, to learn its rhythm, and maybe—just maybe—add to it subtly once you're trusted. In Japan, patience really is a virtue, and as a foreigner, you have to be willing to earn your credibility inch by inch.

## How Foreigners Can Navigate the Senpai-Kouhai System

FOR AN OUTSIDER, THE *senpai-kouhai* structure can be a minefield. It's a fine line between showing respect and completely fading into the background. From my experience, one of the most effective strategies is to actively observe before participating. Even if you're hired for your expertise, Japan values humility in a way that sometimes feels counterintuitive to American sensibilities. Here, it's about finding the right balance—showing initiative without being overly assertive, and learning the art of subtle influence.

One way to navigate this structure is by adopting the *kuchi wo miru* approach—literally, "watching the mouth," or paying attention to how others express themselves. If a *senpai* offers guidance, listen carefully, not just to the words but to the implications behind them. Often, advice here is indirect, and following through without pushing back demonstrates respect. This doesn't mean suppressing your ideas entirely; it means presenting them in a way that acknowledges the *senpai's* position. Think of it as offering a suggestion rather than a solution.

Another tactic is to show an active willingness to learn. In Japan, the *kouhai* role is seen as an important period of growth, and a foreigner who respects this phase—without trying to rush through it—gains credibility. Once, after a long meeting where I held back far more than I was used to, a Japanese colleague commended me for my restraint, saying, "You've adapted well." It was subtle, but in Japanese corporate culture, that's the equivalent of a standing ovation.

Finally, don't underestimate the power of gratitude. A simple gesture like acknowledging the *senpai's* guidance, or a quick word of thanks after they've helped you navigate a tricky situation, goes a long way. In the U.S., we might not think twice about saying "thank you" as a matter of politeness, but in Japan, gratitude is often deeply felt and remembered. It reinforces the sense of loyalty and respect that underpins the *senpai-kouhai* dynamic.

## Finding Opportunities within the Hierarchy

THOUGH THE *senpai-kouhai* structure might seem like a limitation, there's a surprising amount of room to maneuver—if you know how to play the game. For one, once you've established a relationship with your *senpai*, you're often afforded a certain level of protection. In Japan, your *senpai* is almost like a sponsor, someone who'll advocate for you within the company. That advocacy can be priceless, especially for a foreigner who might otherwise struggle to break into the inner circle.

I've seen talented foreign professionals leverage their relationships with *senpai* to great advantage. Once trust is established, a *senpai* can become a sounding board, a coach, and even a guide for navigating the complexities of the Japanese workplace. It's a gradual process, but if you're patient and show respect for the hierarchy, you can eventually earn a voice within the system.

# Chapter 4: Politeness vs. Sincerity: The Duality of Japanese Courtesy

## Tatemae vs. Honne: The Public Face and Private Self

In Japanese culture, there's a concept that every seasoned foreign executive needs to grasp: *tatemae* and *honne*. *Tatemae* refers to the public facade, the mask one wears in social settings, while *honne* represents one's true feelings. This isn't just reserved for personal relationships—*tatemae* is deeply embedded in professional interactions. I learned early on that, in Japan, what's said aloud and what's truly felt can be worlds apart. For an American, raised to "speak one's mind" and encouraged to offer frank feedback, this duality can be perplexing, even frustrating.

I remember a particular business dinner with a Japanese partner company, during which my Japanese counterpart was all smiles and nods. He agreed enthusiastically with every suggestion we presented. I thought we were in sync, that we'd laid the groundwork for a solid partnership. But when the follow-up emails came, they were vague, almost evasive. We'd clearly missed the mark somewhere, but there was no direct feedback—just polite pleasantries and gentle "suggestions." It took a Japanese colleague to explain that the nodding at dinner was *tatemae*, a polite mask to maintain harmony during the meal. Behind that, his *honne*, his true thoughts, had been more cautious.

This was my initiation into the subtle world of Japanese courtesy, where "yes" doesn't always mean yes, and "no" is almost never spoken outright. In a U.S. boardroom, if someone nods, you assume they're on board. In Japan, a nod could mean any number of things—often "I understand what you're saying," rather than "I agree." It's an art of reading between the lines, of understanding that even polite words can hold hesitation or dissent. And as much as it requires patience, it also asks for sensitivity to nuance.

One of my colleagues had an even sharper lesson in *tatemae* during his first project in Tokyo. After weeks of meticulous planning, he presented his strategy to the Japanese team, expecting at least some back-and-forth on specifics. Instead, he was met with what he thought was enthusiastic agreement. They approved the plan, thanked him, and promised to "move forward." But a month later, when he checked in, he discovered that they'd quietly shelved half his ideas. What he hadn't realised was that their approval had been a formality—a way to save face, even though they had little intention of implementing his suggestions.

These situations aren't uncommon. To a Japanese team, it's often more respectful to go along with a senior or foreign colleague's ideas in person and adjust quietly afterward. From their perspective, *tatemae* maintains harmony, especially in interactions where open disagreement might be seen as impolite. It's not deception—it's a courtesy. The true discussion often happens behind closed doors, where *honne* surfaces among colleagues who feel free to express reservations.

This balance between *tatemae* and *honne* isn't something you can decode overnight. For most foreigners, it's a slow process of learning to listen to the silences, the pauses, and even the body language. If someone says, "That may be difficult," it's usually a polite way of saying, "No." And if they say, "Let's look into it," it can mean, "This isn't a priority." I once joked that the best way to navigate *tatemae* and *honne* is to assume every "yes" has an invisible asterisk. You're rarely being outright misled, but you're not always being given the whole picture, either.

# Why Japanese Politeness Is Often Misinterpreted

THIS DUALITY OF PUBLIC and private sentiment means that Japanese politeness can often be mistaken for sincerity. It's easy for a foreigner to walk away from a conversation thinking they've secured a deal or won someone's approval when, in fact, they've only received polite acknowledgment. I've seen it happen countless times: a new manager is thrilled with what seems like a positive response from a Japanese team, only to be disappointed later when the "approval" unravels into ambiguity.

A friend of mine from Chicago, who'd just taken a high-level post in Tokyo, once shared his frustration with me over lunch. He'd been trying to implement a new workflow that he believed would streamline operations. The Japanese team was nothing but polite, giving him encouraging nods and going through the motions. He was convinced he'd won them over—until he noticed they were sticking to their old methods. They never openly opposed him; they simply gave his plan polite lip service, then went right back to the familiar. For them, maintaining harmony by avoiding direct confrontation was more important than expressing their concerns outright.

This tendency for politeness can often leave foreign managers in the dark, scrambling to understand what went wrong. In Western business, a nod or a verbal affirmation is usually a commitment. In Japan, though, it's more complex—a nod is often a sign of understanding rather than agreement, and an affirmation is often a means to avoid conflict, not a promise to follow through. You can imagine how many Western managers have misinterpreted Japanese politeness as genuine buy-in, only to find themselves chasing elusive goals or confused by a lack of follow-up.

For an American, used to direct answers and clear intentions, this can be deeply frustrating. But for the Japanese, bluntness disrupts harmony; it's a ripple in the pond. I've learned to consider politeness as a protective buffer, a means of allowing the other person to "save face" even if they disagree. In time, I learned to read between the lines, to take polite phrases as signals rather than as actual commitments. It's like navigating a maze with subtle markers—if you look carefully, the signs are all there, but they're rarely obvious.

## Nonverbal Communication and Subtle Cues

PERHAPS EVEN MORE INTRICATE than *tatemae* and *honne* is the Japanese reliance on nonverbal communication. If you're attuned to the subtleties, Japanese body language can tell you what words won't. A slight pause before a nod, a soft "mmm" in response to a suggestion, or even the way someone pours your tea can communicate more than any spoken words. These unspoken cues are where you'll find the truth of *honne*, the genuine feelings lurking behind *tatemae*.

One of my early encounters with this was with a Japanese partner who rarely gave direct answers. He'd respond with a quiet nod, a thoughtful pause, and then maybe a low "soudesune..." which translates loosely to "I see" or "That's so." At first, I thought he was agreeing, that he was on board with our proposal. But over time, I picked up on the hesitation in his voice, the way he'd carefully avoid committing. That "soudesune" was more of a polite placeholder, a respectful "I hear you" rather than an enthusiastic endorsement.

In one memorable meeting, I presented a project that required significant changes in workflow. My Japanese counterpart nodded, murmured "naruhodo," meaning "I see" or "That makes sense," and gave what I thought was an encouraging smile. But something felt off. He was looking down, fidgeting slightly, and his voice had softened in a way that seemed uncertain. It was only later, in a private conversation with one of his colleagues, that I learned he'd had reservations about the plan all along but hadn't felt comfortable voicing them directly.

In the States, hesitation usually comes with a frown or some vocal pushback. Here, it's softer, more controlled. A hesitation, a pause, or a lack of eye contact are the ways discomfort surfaces. For someone used to reading verbal cues, this unspoken language can be a minefield. I had to learn that even a polite smile could mean disagreement, and a nod could be a way of keeping the peace rather than indicating acceptance.

The key is to watch carefully and listen even more closely. It's a skill, learning to interpret these cues, and it's one that's rarely mastered quickly. Once, after a particularly successful meeting, I remember thinking I'd finally broken through, only to learn later that the team was still uncertain. My American colleague, who'd joined me on the project, laughed and said, "They're too nice to just say no!" He wasn't wrong. Sometimes, you have to train yourself to "hear" what isn't said, to watch for those subtle shifts that reveal true intent.

## The Impact of Politeness on Workplace Feedback and Criticism

WHEN I FIRST STARTED working in Japan, I was caught off guard by how feedback was delivered. In the U.S., feedback is often straightforward, sometimes even blunt. If your idea doesn't hold water, you're likely to hear about it then and there. In Japan, however, feedback is wrapped in so many layers of courtesy that it can be easy to miss the criticism altogether. I remember one of my first meetings with our local team—Paul, a British colleague, and I were presenting a new workflow that we thought would boost efficiency. Everyone nodded and smiled, but something felt off. No one asked questions or raised concerns, which struck me as odd for such a big change.

After the meeting, John, a senior member of the Japanese team, approached me. With a gentle smile, he said, "Danny-san, there are perhaps some areas we could consider improving." His tone was so mild, I almost brushed it off as a casual suggestion. But as I later learned from Nancy, our American HR manager, that was John's way of hinting that there were serious issues with our proposal. "In Japan, they'll rarely come out and say it directly," she explained. "You've got to read between the lines." It was a lesson that has stayed with me.

In Japanese culture, direct criticism is considered impolite, especially if it might cause someone to "lose face." So, when a Japanese colleague says, "It might be difficult to implement," what they often mean is, "I don't think this will work." For someone like Paul, who was used to clear, actionable feedback, it was frustrating at first. "How am I supposed to improve if I don't even know what's wrong?" he'd complain. But over time, we both learned that in Japan, understanding the nuances of polite feedback is essential. The onus is on the listener to pick up on subtle cues, a skill that feels almost like reading a new language.

Nancy, who had worked in Japan for over a decade, became something of a cultural translator for us. She'd sit in on meetings and decode the polite phrases and body language, pointing out when "maybe" actually meant "no." Once, after a project review, she turned to me and said, "When Yuki kept saying 'that might be challenging,' she meant it's a flat-out 'no.' Trust me." This level of subtlety was hard for Westerners to wrap their heads around, especially for Paul, who preferred straightforward instructions. But over time, I started to appreciate the elegance in Japanese feedback—how it allowed you to save face, even if your idea was being politely dismissed.

## Navigating Japanese Courtesy as a Foreigner

FOR FOREIGNERS, LEARNING to navigate Japanese politeness is both a challenge and a rite of passage. Japanese politeness is designed to avoid friction, which is admirable, but it can also be a minefield for the uninitiated. I remember Paul once told me, half-jokingly, "Danny, I think I'd understand Japanese business better if they just yelled at me." He was exaggerating, of course, but there was a truth to it. For those of us used to direct communication, Japan's indirect approach felt like a puzzle.

One time, we were discussing a new marketing campaign, and I could tell that something wasn't sitting right with our Japanese team. I glanced over at John, who seemed unusually quiet, and realised he hadn't said a word of feedback. When I asked him for his thoughts afterward, he politely replied, "It's a very creative approach." For a moment, I took that as approval. But then I remembered Nancy's advice: Japanese feedback, when positive, tends to be effusive. A simple "creative" usually means they're being polite. Sure enough, the campaign quietly fizzled out after several rounds of "polite" adjustments.

As foreigners, we had to train ourselves to ask indirect questions to elicit more genuine responses. Instead of saying, "Do you like this idea?" I learned to ask, "What areas could we improve?" Or, "Do you think this might cause any challenges?" These open-ended questions give Japanese colleagues the chance to voice concerns without feeling they're directly contradicting someone. Nancy was the first to adopt this approach and taught us that we needed to provide a "safe space" for feedback. Otherwise, Japanese team members would revert to the default *tatemae*, and we'd leave thinking everyone was on board when they weren't.

Over time, I realised that understanding Japanese politeness was less about figuring out what people *weren't* saying, and more about creating an environment where they felt comfortable saying what they *wanted* to say. It's not a foolproof system, and there are still moments when I misinterpret polite responses, but I've come to appreciate the thoughtfulness behind it. The Japanese see politeness as a way to maintain harmony, even if that means sacrificing a little directness. For someone like Paul, who started out bristling at the lack of forthright feedback, it was a revelation. "They're not trying to confuse us," he told me after one successful project, "they're trying to be considerate."

## The Role of Politeness in Professional

# Networking and Trust-Building

IN JAPAN, POLITENESS isn't just a social nicety—it's the bedrock of professional relationships. If you can navigate this duality of courtesy and sincerity, you'll find that Japanese colleagues will slowly begin to open up, sharing their true thoughts more freely. I learned this first-hand with a client named Sato-san, a reserved but respected senior executive in Tokyo. At first, Sato-san's responses were the same polite affirmations I'd come to expect. He'd smile, nod, and offer vague encouragements, but nothing concrete. But after months of consistent, respectful follow-ups, I noticed a shift.

During a particularly tricky negotiation, Sato-san leaned over to me and quietly suggested an approach that wasn't in our plan. "Perhaps, Danny-san, it might be more effective if we present this differently," he whispered, almost conspiratorially. It was a small breakthrough, but it marked a turning point in our working relationship. From then on, his feedback became less guarded, his "yes" and "no" clearer. It was as though I'd earned the privilege of his *honne*, his true thoughts, after proving I could be trusted with his *tatemae*.

Nancy also emphasised that Japanese networking doesn't happen in the boardroom; it often happens over drinks. She would tell us, "If you want to build trust, you have to embrace the *nomikai* culture." These after-hours gatherings are where formality fades, and genuine conversations begin. I remember one such evening, sitting in a tiny izakaya with John, Paul, and our Japanese counterparts. After a few rounds of sake, the polite facades dropped just a bit. Our Japanese colleagues started to share openly, cracking jokes and offering feedback without the usual layers of courtesy.

Paul, who had struggled most with Japanese indirectness, was surprised by how candid everyone became. "All this time, I thought they were just being difficult," he whispered to me. But the truth is, Japanese politeness is like a gate—you have to go through it first, show respect, and then, slowly, you're granted access to a more genuine level of communication. By the end of the night, even John, our most reserved Japanese colleague, was sharing stories of his career struggles and advice on navigating Japanese corporate politics.

Building these relationships doesn't happen overnight. It takes time, patience, and a willingness to embrace their rules of politeness. But once you understand it, the rewards are significant. For all the complexity, Japanese politeness offers a way to connect deeply—if you're willing to learn its nuances. Paul, who initially found it frustrating, came to appreciate it as much as I did. "It's not about getting to the truth right away," he told me one evening after a *nomikai*. "It's about earning it."

By understanding *tatemae* and *honne*, learning to read the subtle cues, and embracing the role of politeness in Japanese professional life, we eventually found our footing. Japanese courtesy may be layered, but once you learn the steps, it leads to a trust and loyalty that are hard to find elsewhere. For me, navigating this duality of politeness and sincerity has been a journey of discovery, and one that's made me value my Japanese colleagues even more.

# Chapter 5: The Importance of Harmony (Wa) and Conformity in Daily Interactions

In Japan, the concept of *wa*—harmony—is more than just a cultural ideal; it's the cornerstone of nearly every social and professional interaction. Maintaining *wa* is often considered more important than personal opinions, even if it means holding back feedback, ideas, or criticism. For a foreign executive, it's a challenge to balance their usual directness with Japan's need for equilibrium. For my team and me—folks like Paul, John, and Nancy—it took time to understand that getting things done wasn't just about getting buy-in or reaching consensus; it was about preserving *wa* every step of the way.

## Wa as the Foundation of Japanese Social Order

ONE OF THE FIRST THINGS I noticed in Japanese business culture was that conflicts aren't usually addressed head-on; instead, they're managed quietly, almost invisibly. *Wa* isn't just a concept—it's a practice woven into every aspect of Japanese professional life. In Japan, keeping the peace is paramount, and you'll often find that individuals will go out of their way to avoid disrupting the group harmony. This emphasis on *wa* influences everything from the structure of meetings to how people address one another.

Early on, I sat in on a meeting between my colleague Paul and a Japanese department head named Yuki. We were discussing a proposal that Paul had prepared, but I could sense that Yuki wasn't fully convinced. He nodded politely, asked a few questions, and offered what appeared to be a warm smile. I assumed he was on board. After the meeting, however, a Japanese colleague quietly mentioned that Yuki's silence was a sign of discomfort, that he was reluctant to criticize openly because doing so might disrupt the harmony of the group. Paul had taken Yuki's silence as agreement, when in fact, it was an indication of disapproval masked by a polite exterior.

It was a stark reminder: while directness might work well in the West, in Japan, even the most subtle dissonance can be seen as a disruption. Respecting *wa* meant that we, as foreigners, needed to recalibrate our approach, learning to read between the lines to gauge when harmony was being preserved—and when it was at risk.

## Groupthink: When Conformity Overrides Individual Input

CONFORMITY IN JAPAN goes beyond simple teamwork; it's a deep-seated norm that promotes unity but can sometimes stifle individual expression. This is particularly evident in the concept of *nemawashi*, a term that means "laying the groundwork." Before a decision is made in a meeting, it's common for discussions to take place informally, ensuring that everyone is aligned before presenting it to the wider group. This pre-alignment, while efficient in avoiding conflict, can limit the breadth of ideas that surface.

John, who was used to openly challenging ideas, found this particularly difficult. He once voiced a different approach during a planning session, suggesting an unconventional strategy. The reaction? Polite nods, but little enthusiasm. Later, a Japanese colleague explained to him, "John-san, it is best if we discuss changes in private first, so everyone is comfortable when it's brought up publicly." Essentially, John's eagerness to contribute his ideas directly clashed with the team's preference for quiet, collective agreement.

I saw that groupthink, reinforced by the importance of *wa*, wasn't just about agreement for its own sake. It was a mechanism to protect everyone's face and maintain the comfort level of the group. For foreigners like John, understanding that ideas often needed to be shared in private conversations before being introduced in formal meetings was a crucial shift. It wasn't that his ideas weren't valued; they just had to be presented in a way that preserved the group's equilibrium.

## The Consequences of Challenging Wa

BREAKING *wa* in Japan isn't taken lightly, and those who do can find themselves subtly, or even overtly, sidelined. I once witnessed Nancy experience this firsthand. She'd grown frustrated with what she saw as inefficiencies in the local team's workflow and decided to address them head-on in a team meeting. "We need to streamline this process," she'd said, proposing a quicker, more efficient method. The room went quiet, and I could feel the tension rising as her Japanese counterparts exchanged glances. Nancy's direct approach, while logical and efficient, had unintentionally disrupted *wa* by suggesting that the team's current practices were flawed.

Over the next few weeks, she noticed that her Japanese colleagues were more guarded around her, giving her short, polite answers but avoiding in-depth collaboration. Her well-intentioned feedback had inadvertently marked her as someone willing to disrupt the harmony of the team, making others wary of engaging too deeply with her. It was a lesson she took to heart. After that experience, she began couching her suggestions more gently, often framing them as questions rather than directives. Slowly, the team warmed up again, and Nancy learned the subtle art of maintaining *wa* while still contributing her ideas.

# Practical Tips for Foreigners to Maintain Wa

TO RESPECT *wa* as a foreigner, it's essential to approach interactions with an understanding that harmony often comes first. Here are a few lessons I picked up over the years:

**1 Check in Privately**: Before bringing up a new idea, consult privately with Japanese colleagues. This allows them to express concerns or reservations candidly, without feeling pressured in a public setting. It's a way of doing *nemawashi*, and it shows respect for the consensus-driven culture.

**2 Frame Suggestions as Questions**: Instead of saying, "We should do this differently," try, "Do you think there might be another way to approach this?" This indirect approach invites input and preserves harmony, showing that you're not imposing but suggesting.

**3 Watch for Nonverbal Cues**: In Japan, body language is key. A slight pause or a hesitant nod often signals disagreement or discomfort. When in doubt, follow up one-on-one to clarify any ambiguities.

**4 Appreciate Their Efforts**: Compliments go a long way in Japan. Acknowledge the team's work before introducing changes. Recognising their effort maintains *wa* and softens the impact of your suggestions.

These practices might seem subtle, but they make a significant difference in maintaining the flow of *wa* and building trust among Japanese colleagues.

# Balancing Individuality and Conformity in Multinational Teams

NAVIGATING *wa* in a multinational team is about finding a middle ground between respecting the group's comfort and introducing outside perspectives. Japanese teams tend to value consensus, which sometimes means sacrificing speed or innovation for stability. I saw this tension play out with Paul during a high-stakes project involving both Japanese and Western teams. Paul's approach was efficient and results-driven, but he quickly realised that his Japanese counterparts valued careful, measured progress over fast results.

For the Japanese team, every decision needed to be thoroughly vetted to avoid missteps, even if it meant slowing down the pace. Paul learned that by showing a willingness to work within this system—being patient and showing respect for their process—he could eventually bring his ideas to the table without disrupting the flow. It took time, but by prioritising *wa*, he found that his suggestions were better received, and his rapport with the team grew stronger.

In the end, balancing individuality and conformity is a give-and-take. Foreigners who respect *wa* often find that their ideas gain traction once they've demonstrated an understanding of Japanese values. In this way, *wa* becomes not an obstacle but a guide—a framework that, if respected, can open doors.

## How Wa Affects Innovation and Decision-Making

THERE'S A PERCEPTION in Western business circles that *wa* stifles innovation, that Japan's emphasis on harmony prevents fresh ideas from taking root. But that's not entirely accurate. While *wa* can slow down decision-making, it also means that when a consensus is reached, everyone is fully on board. There's no second-guessing, no backtracking—just a solid commitment to move forward as a united front.

John once pointed this out after a challenging project. "In the U.S., we'd be halfway done by now," he mused, "but everyone would be complaining about the process." In Japan, the time spent reaching consensus is seen as an investment. It ensures that when action is finally taken, the team moves in harmony, reducing conflicts or issues down the line. For John, this was a revelation: while the Japanese process might seem slow, it was highly effective in ensuring stability.

Over time, I've come to appreciate the resilience of *wa* and the balance it brings. It might ask for patience, but in return, it fosters an environment where colleagues work together, fully aligned. In the West, we often rush for results; in Japan, they cultivate *wa*, trusting that the results will follow. It's a profound difference, and one that has taught me the value of patience, respect, and collective purpose in the workplace.

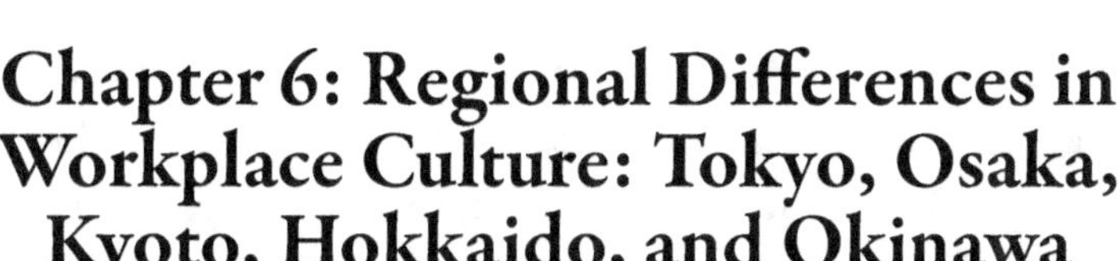

# Chapter 6: Regional Differences in Workplace Culture: Tokyo, Osaka, Kyoto, Hokkaido, and Okinawa

One of the most fascinating aspects of working in Japan is realising that "Japanese culture" isn't a one-size-fits-all concept. Just as the U.S. has its own distinct regional flavours, from New York's fast-paced style to the laid-back West Coast approach, Japan's work culture varies across its regions. Each city and region has its own tempo, attitudes, and unspoken rules that shape interactions in unique ways. Tokyo's polished formality, Osaka's directness, Kyoto's reserved manner, Hokkaido's relaxed openness, and Okinawa's island-time friendliness all bring different flavours to the workplace. Understanding these regional differences can make all the difference in forging strong, meaningful professional relationships.

## Tokyo: Formality and Efficiency

WHEN PEOPLE THINK OF Japan's business culture, Tokyo's corporate style often sets the standard. It's the business hub of the country, and everything here is done with a certain level of formality and polish. The Tokyo office culture feels almost like a machine—well-organised, polite, and extremely efficient. If you're stepping into a meeting in Tokyo, be prepared for a meticulously structured agenda, a clear hierarchy, and a sense of gravitas that feels almost ceremonial.

I remember when Nancy and I first started working with our Tokyo counterparts, she commented on how different it felt from our previous assignments in Osaka. "It's like everything here has to be picture-perfect," she said, noting the way employees bowed precisely, delivered presentations flawlessly, and kept a strict adherence to protocol. In Tokyo, appearances matter. People dress a little sharper, conversations are a touch more reserved, and respect for hierarchy is unwavering. Even casual small talk is kept to a minimum, reserved for breaks rather than the meeting room.

One of my first impressions of Tokyo was how everyone seemed to be on their best behaviour, almost as if the stakes were higher here. A simple misstep—arriving late to a meeting, or misinterpreting a senior colleague's request—felt weightier, as though Tokyo's standards didn't allow room for error. Here, professionalism and formality create a veneer of composure that might feel rigid to an outsider, but it's also highly efficient. You know where you stand, who's in charge, and what's expected of you. But beneath this formality, Tokyo's professionals are pragmatic, and once they trust you, they'll appreciate directness—though delivered with respect.

## Osaka: Directness and Hospitality in Business

IN OSAKA, THE ENERGY couldn't be more different. If Tokyo is formal and reserved, Osaka is vibrant and direct. Osaka has a reputation for being the friendlier, more down-to-earth sibling to Tokyo, and it shows in the workplace culture. People here are refreshingly candid, and they're not afraid to laugh or crack a joke during a meeting—something you wouldn't often find in Tokyo. In Osaka, colleagues are more likely to speak their minds, and there's a certain "what you see is what you get" attitude that feels almost liberating compared to Tokyo's restrained approach.

One of my first experiences with Osaka's style was during a project kickoff. I was getting into my formal mode, expecting the same structured protocol as in Tokyo, when one of the senior managers interrupted me mid-sentence to offer an alternate perspective. "No offense, Danny-san," he said with a grin, "but we do things a little differently here." It was said with such warmth that I couldn't help but smile. Here, disagreements aren't swept under the rug—they're out in the open, and they're handled with a sense of humour.

Paul, who had initially found Japan's indirect communication challenging, felt right at home in Osaka. "Finally, people who say what they mean!" he joked. But that doesn't mean Osaka lacks professionalism. There's a strong work ethic here, but it's coupled with a sense of hospitality that's unique to the region. People are willing to spend extra time helping a colleague or making sure a foreign guest feels at ease. Business dinners in Osaka are lively affairs, where discussions blend work and personal stories over good food and drinks, building a rapport that Tokyo's formality often precludes. It's a place where relationships are built on openness, humour, and a hearty "let's get it done" attitude.

## Kyoto: Tradition and Caution in Decision-Making

KYOTO, JAPAN'S ANCIENT capital, carries its cultural heritage into its workplace dynamics. There's a saying that in Kyoto, people "smile with their stomach," meaning that politeness and true feelings may not always align. In Kyoto's business world, the past is always present, and interactions tend to be more reserved and layered with subtlety. Here, there's a cautious approach to everything, as though every action is weighed for its impact on tradition and reputation.

During one project in Kyoto, I was struck by how the decision-making process felt slower, more deliberate. Proposals went through multiple rounds of review, and feedback came at a glacial pace. Nancy explained it best when she said, "Kyoto's about respect—not just for people, but for process." You don't just pitch an idea and expect an immediate response. Instead, you let it settle, wait for it to circulate, and trust that, if it's valuable, it will gain traction in time.

There's a certain elegance to Kyoto's approach. Meetings are often quieter, with more pauses and reflective silences. People listen carefully, and you're unlikely to see the same level of direct engagement that's common in Osaka. Kyoto businesspeople value tradition, so change is introduced with care. I learned to adapt by framing my suggestions with references to past successes, showing respect for the legacy of the company or industry. Kyoto isn't about rushing into the future—it's about building on the past, step by careful step.

## Hokkaido: A Relaxed Openness in Business Culture

HOKKAIDO, JAPAN'S NORTHERNMOST island, is known for its rugged landscapes and its people's resilience. Workplace culture here is more relaxed and approachable, with a stronger sense of camaraderie. People in Hokkaido are known for their openness, a characteristic that extends into their professional lives. The Hokkaido workplace feels less hierarchical and formal than Tokyo or Kyoto, and there's a spirit of cooperation that reflects the region's sense of community.

When John and I first visited Hokkaido for a client meeting, we were struck by how casual the environment was. Unlike the strict schedules and formal attire of Tokyo, our hosts in Hokkaido were less concerned with appearances and more focused on substance. People here speak their minds, but in a softer, more unassuming way than in Osaka. The pace is slower, and there's less pressure to conform to a rigid hierarchy.

In Hokkaido, you're more likely to have a brainstorming session outdoors or find that people are keen to invite you to local festivals and events. Business here is less about power suits and more about relationships and trust. If Tokyo's interactions feel like a well-choreographed dance, Hokkaido's are more like a conversation around a campfire—casual, open, and sincere. For someone used to Japan's urban intensity, Hokkaido offers a refreshing contrast, a place where work feels like an extension of community life.

## Okinawa and Rural Japan: Island-Time Friendliness and Flexibility

OKINAWA, JAPAN'S SOUTHERNMOST prefecture, and other rural regions bring their own unique spin to workplace culture. Okinawans have a reputation for friendliness and flexibility, a stark contrast to Tokyo's meticulousness or Kyoto's formality. This island-time mindset means that deadlines are more fluid, and work-life balance is a higher priority. In Okinawa, there's an openness and warmth that feels almost tropical, a natural reflection of the island's slower, more relaxed pace.

In Okinawa, I found that business meetings were often blended with social gatherings. People are eager to share their local culture and stories, and they take pride in fostering a sense of family within the workplace. It's a region where hierarchy is respected, but it's more relaxed, and the barriers between senior and junior staff are softer. Okinawans value harmony, but they're also open to outside ideas, especially when those ideas are presented in a spirit of collaboration rather than disruption.

This openness is common in many of Japan's rural areas, where the pace of life is slower and people value personal relationships as much as professional ones. I remember a conversation in rural Kyushu, "In the countryside, we work together because we live together." That sentiment shapes the workplace, making it more of a cooperative effort than a competitive one. People are willing to lend a hand, share advice, and take their time to make sure everyone is on the same page.

For Paul, who was accustomed to Tokyo's structured intensity, Okinawa and rural Japan were eye-opening experiences. "It's like a different country," he once remarked. And in many ways, he was right. While Tokyo operates at a breakneck pace, Okinawa's culture gives room for flexibility, showing that Japan's work culture isn't just one thing—it's a tapestry of local traditions, each with its own way of balancing productivity with the values of the region.

## Navigating Regional Differences as a Foreigner

AS A FOREIGNER, UNDERSTANDING these regional differences can be crucial. Tokyo's formality, Osaka's directness, Kyoto's caution, Hokkaido's openness, and Okinawa's friendliness each present unique challenges and opportunities. In Tokyo, it pays to be precise and polished; in Osaka, a little humour goes a long way. In Kyoto, patience and respect for tradition will earn you allies, while in Hokkaido and Okinawa, sincerity and a willingness to connect personally can open doors that might otherwise remain closed.

One memorable example involved Paul during a joint venture meeting in Osaka. He'd adjusted his approach after learning the value of Osaka's more open, friendly business style, and it worked wonders. Instead of diving straight into the logistics, he started the meeting with a casual conversation, sharing a light-hearted story about his last visit to Osaka. The Osaka team responded with laughter, and it set a comfortable tone for the rest of the session. It was one of those moments where the direct, no-nonsense energy of Osaka matched perfectly with his style. If Paul had tried this in Tokyo or Kyoto, it might have come across as unprofessional or overly familiar, but here, it built immediate rapport.

Nancy had a contrasting experience during a project in Kyoto. She presented a proposal with enthusiasm, highlighting its potential benefits. Yet, the room was quiet, and everyone looked contemplative. Nancy admitted afterward that she'd felt awkward, as if she'd said something amiss. But over the following days, she started receiving feedback through indirect channels—emails with polite suggestions, comments shared by colleagues who had spoken with others in the team. Kyoto's reserved approach, she realised, was their way of carefully weighing new ideas without rushing to judgment. She adapted by presenting her ideas in a more understated way, allowing them to sink in over time rather than pushing for immediate agreement.

I found Hokkaido to be one of the most comfortable regions for foreigners to adapt to, with its welcoming and straightforward approach. During my time there, I often found people to be less concerned with rigid formality and more focused on building genuine connections. The team I worked with had an openness that made it easier to ask questions and clarify expectations. There was a refreshing simplicity to Hokkaido's interactions—business was still professional, but the tone was relaxed. My colleagues there shared information freely, rarely held back on feedback, and took the time to explain cultural nuances in ways that didn't leave me guessing.

Okinawa brought its own unique experience, with a friendliness that was both welcoming and deceptively informal. One thing I quickly learned was that schedules here were more flexible, and deadlines felt less rigid. In one instance, a local project manager suggested we "relax" over lunch to discuss an issue. I was taken aback, expecting a formal, sit-down meeting, but instead found myself enjoying a casual, open conversation that covered both work and local insights. This relaxed approach didn't mean a lack of professionalism; it was simply a reflection of the island's cultural emphasis on relationships. Over time, I realised that in Okinawa, strong relationships often led to a natural trust, which in turn facilitated smoother business dealings.

Each of these regions shaped my understanding of Japan's multifaceted business culture, but it was the ability to adapt to these variations that made me, and my team, more effective in our roles. It became clear that knowing the right approach wasn't about following a fixed strategy—it was about being flexible, reading the room, and matching the style of the people we were working with. For a foreigner, the more adaptable you are to these regional nuances, the easier it becomes to earn respect and achieve meaningful results in Japan.

In the end, Japan's regional diversity in workplace culture taught us all valuable lessons. Tokyo's professionalism, Osaka's warmth, Kyoto's reverence for tradition, Hokkaido's openness, and Okinawa's friendliness each have something unique to offer. When working across Japan, embracing these differences isn't just beneficial—it's essential. Every city, every office has its own rhythm, and knowing how to move with it can mean the difference between being just another foreigner and becoming a respected partner.

# Part 3: The Unspoken Rules and Common Complaints of the Japanese Workplace

# Chapter 7: Case Study – A Foreigner's First Day in a Japanese Office

Stepping into a Japanese office for the first time can be a bewildering experience, especially for those of us used to a more casual, often fast-paced Western approach. The structure, the quiet intensity, and the small rituals can make it feel as though you've entered another world. To navigate it successfully, it's crucial to understand the subtleties at play and how to interpret what isn't being said. I remember my own first day in Tokyo, walking into an office where everyone seemed to know exactly where they stood. While I was accustomed to collaboration from the start, here, there was a palpable sense of hierarchy and formality.

A foreigner's first day isn't just about fitting into a team—it's about making a lasting impression. The Japanese office environment operates on an unspoken expectation: that every new team member, especially a foreigner, will respect and observe these long-standing practices. You're being watched, assessed, not just for your competence but for your ability to respect Japanese norms and traditions. So here's what I learned, along with a few practical tips for how to survive—and thrive—in this new environment.

## The Morning Ritual: Arriving Early but Not Too Early

IN JAPAN, PUNCTUALITY is everything. On my first day, I was advised to arrive at least fifteen minutes early, a buffer that showed respect without coming across as overeager. Showing up too early could inconvenience your colleagues, while arriving even a minute late could damage your reputation. Japan's approach to time is disciplined, and your punctuality is viewed as a reflection of your character and respect for others.

When I arrived, I made sure to greet the receptionist with a small bow and a polite "ohayou gozaimasu" (good morning). I'd practiced the phrase a few times the night before, wanting to get the pronunciation just right. While it might seem like a small gesture, taking the time to speak Japanese—even if it's just a greeting—signifies that you're making an effort to fit in, and that goes a long way.

## Understanding Seating Arrangements and Hierarchical Nuances

ONE OF THE FIRST THINGS you'll notice in a Japanese office is the importance of seating arrangements. In meeting rooms, seats are assigned according to rank, with the highest-ranking person seated at the "top" of the table, often farthest from the door. Your seat isn't random; it reflects your role in the meeting. On that first day, I was placed near the door, a subtle way of reminding me that I was a newcomer. Observing this hierarchy from the get-go is crucial—it's a system that runs deep and speaks volumes about each person's place within the organisation.

If you're unsure where to sit, a safe bet is to wait until others are seated or ask a colleague where they'd like you to sit. Trust me, this small gesture of deference can make a huge difference. When my colleague Nancy joined her team in Kyoto, she mistakenly took a seat meant for a senior manager. It was a minor slip, but it created an awkward moment, one that could have been avoided with a simple question.

# The First Meeting: The Art of Listening and Observing

ON THAT FIRST DAY, my initial meeting with the team was an exercise in patience. Meetings in Japan often involve a lot of listening, and new hires—especially foreigners—are expected to listen more than they speak. This isn't the time to jump in with your ideas or suggestions; it's a chance to observe the team's dynamics, who speaks, who remains silent, and how decisions are made. Your colleagues are watching how you handle this too, evaluating your respect for the group dynamic.

For a foreigner, this listening-first approach might feel frustrating, especially if you're used to being proactive. But showing restraint is key. In Japan, speaking out too soon can be interpreted as a lack of humility or, worse, an unwillingness to adapt. When my colleague John took the initiative during his first meeting in Osaka, his enthusiasm was met with polite nods but also a few glances that signaled mild disapproval. Later, a Japanese colleague advised him to "listen first, contribute second." He adjusted quickly and found that his ideas were more warmly received once he'd taken the time to understand the team's style.

# How to Handle Feedback: Taking Notes and Showing Respect

FEEDBACK IN JAPAN ISN'T always as straightforward as it is in the West. Often, it's given in roundabout ways or through indirect language. On my first day, I made it a point to carry a notebook, jotting down every piece of advice, every observation, and even the small talk shared by my colleagues. Taking notes, especially during meetings or when receiving feedback, is seen as a mark of respect here. It shows that you're attentive, diligent, and taking your role seriously.

At one point, my manager suggested that "perhaps" a different approach "might be useful," a phrase that's typically code for "change your approach." I've since learned that this indirect language is a way of protecting both parties' dignity, but on that first day, it took some getting used to. My advice for any foreigner: Don't assume the feedback is as mild as it sounds. If you're being advised to "consider" an alternative, it's likely that your initial idea wasn't well-received. Adapt and show appreciation for the guidance—it will earn you respect and help you integrate faster.

## After-Hours Expectations: The Nomikai

IN JAPAN, AFTER-HOURS gatherings, or *nomikai*, are often just as important as what happens during the workday. If you're invited to a *nomikai*, it's generally seen as an opportunity to bond outside of the rigid office hierarchy. Accepting the invitation, even if you're not particularly keen on drinking, demonstrates a willingness to be part of the team. In my case, I was invited to a *nomikai* that very first evening, and while I was tempted to decline (jet lag was kicking in), I knew that attending was the right choice.

The *nomikai* is a rare setting where hierarchies relax slightly, and people feel freer to express themselves. During that first gathering, I found that colleagues who had been quiet during the day opened up, sharing stories and advice in a much more relaxed way. They even encouraged me to share my background, something they'd shown little interest in during the formal office hours. The experience taught me that these after-hours interactions are an invaluable part of Japanese workplace culture—a space where camaraderie is built, and where people get a sense of who you are beyond your professional role.

If you're unsure how to handle drinking in a *nomikai*, pace yourself. Your colleagues will appreciate it if you join in, but it's perfectly acceptable to nurse a single drink. Just be mindful to keep up with the group's energy, as leaving too early can be seen as a lack of interest in team bonding.

## Reflections: Key Takeaways for Foreigners

LOOKING BACK ON MY first day, I realise that adapting to a Japanese workplace is less about mastering tasks and more about learning the rhythm of the environment. It's about patience, respect, and observing the unspoken rules that make the workplace function smoothly. The biggest mistakes foreigners make are usually from a lack of observation, jumping in too quickly, or not paying attention to the subtleties that matter here.

If I could offer one piece of advice to newcomers, it's this: Spend the first few days simply observing. Take notes, watch how others interact, and show respect through your silence as much as through your words. Learn who the decision-makers are, how feedback is given, and when it's appropriate to speak up. In Japan, understanding the context of a conversation is as important as the content, and adapting to this will not only make your first day easier but will also lay the foundation for successful relationships within the team.

Entering a Japanese office isn't just about joining a new workplace; it's about entering a new world of values and expectations. For a foreigner, understanding these nuances from day one can make the difference between a smooth integration and a career-long cultural disconnect. The key isn't just adapting to Japan's business practices but embracing them fully. After all, a successful day in a Japanese office isn't just about what you accomplish—it's about how you go about it, with a balance of humility, attentiveness, and respect for the traditions that have shaped the culture.

# Chapter 8: Respecting (and Questioning) Authority – The Do's and Don'ts

In a Japanese workplace, authority isn't something you take lightly. Respect for hierarchy is a deeply embedded value, and it's one of the defining characteristics of Japanese corporate culture. If you want to fit in, understanding how to navigate this respect for authority is essential. Every interaction with a superior reflects not just on you but on the harmony of the group. At the same time, questioning authority can be a delicate balancing act—one that requires finesse, timing, and a careful reading of the room.

Unlike in the West, where questioning a manager can be seen as a sign of initiative, in Japan, it's often perceived as disruptive, even presumptuous. But this doesn't mean that you can never offer a different perspective. There's a subtle art to expressing disagreement here, and it's possible to voice your thoughts without breaking the social rules that keep the workplace in harmony. Here are some practical insights into how to respect authority while ensuring your voice is still heard.

## Understanding Authority as Part of the Group Structure

IN JAPAN, THE COMPANY is viewed almost as an extension of family, and within that "family," hierarchy plays a role akin to elder respect. Authority is woven into the structure; it's not about power for its own sake but about maintaining balance and order. This respect for authority means that superiors are rarely questioned outright. Instead, they're given a wide berth, and it's expected that juniors and subordinates will follow their lead with deference.

If you want to fit in, respecting this structure is critical. Superiors don't just expect obedience—they expect you to trust their decisions as an extension of the company's mission. For example, during my time working with a team in Kyoto, I noticed how even minor decisions were deferred to senior managers. At first, this seemed excessive, but I came to understand that it was a way of reinforcing their roles, of showing trust in their experience. In this setting, even if you feel certain that there's a better way, your first instinct should be to respect the established structure.

## The Indirect Approach: Voicing Your Perspective

OF COURSE, THERE ARE times when you may have insights or information that your manager may not be fully aware of. In Japan, bringing up a new idea or perspective doesn't require a full-throttle, direct approach; instead, it's about offering your thoughts as a suggestion, often framed in a way that defers to your superior's expertise. For instance, rather than saying, "I think we should do it this way," a better approach might be, "I wonder if it might be useful to consider this option as well." This phrasing acknowledges your superior's role while subtly introducing your own idea.

John, a colleague of mine who joined the Tokyo office, found this approach especially helpful. He realised that by positioning his ideas as questions or suggestions, he was able to share them without seeming confrontational. "It's almost like planting a seed," he once said to me. "You let the idea sit there, and if it resonates, they'll come back to it." It's a subtle, patient strategy, but one that respects the Japanese workplace's indirect communication style.

This approach allows you to preserve hierarchy while offering a new perspective. In Japan, authority figures appreciate tact; a carefully phrased suggestion shows respect and gives them the opportunity to accept the idea without feeling their authority is being challenged.

## When to Question Authority: Timing Is Everything

IN JAPANESE BUSINESS culture, timing is key. Even the best ideas can be poorly received if brought up at the wrong time. If you're working on a project and feel that there's a need to pivot or reconsider a strategy, it's wise to first wait for an appropriate moment. For example, meetings tend to be a formal environment where decisions are presented rather than debated. So, instead of raising questions or objections in the middle of a meeting, it's often more effective to approach your superior privately afterward.

Nancy, another member of our team, learned this the hard way during a project in Osaka. She raised a concern during a team-wide presentation, hoping to address a potential flaw in the plan. While her intent was well-meaning, the timing disrupted the flow of the meeting. Afterward, her manager gently advised her to share her feedback in a more private setting next time. She took the advice to heart, and from then on, if she had questions, she would find a quieter moment to bring them up one-on-one. Timing her feedback not only preserved her relationship with the team but also gave her thoughts a better chance of being taken seriously.

In Japan, questioning authority openly can be seen as overstepping, especially in a formal setting. Choosing the right moment, often during informal or one-on-one discussions, can make all the difference. It's not just about when you speak, but how you present your ideas to ensure they are received constructively.

# Showing Humility and Acknowledging Hierarchy

IN JAPAN, ACKNOWLEDGING hierarchy isn't just expected; it's respected. If you want to fit in, showing humility is one of the quickest ways to demonstrate your understanding of this expectation. While in Western workplaces we're often taught to emphasise our achievements and promote our expertise, Japanese workplaces reward those who are humble, even self-effacing. You don't need to make yourself smaller, but recognising your place within the structure builds trust.

This practice of humility was something I saw Paul embrace during his time in Kyoto. He'd initially struggled with the idea of not putting his accomplishments front and centre. But he gradually realised that in Japan, humility wasn't seen as a lack of confidence—it was seen as maturity. Rather than asserting himself outright, he began to acknowledge the input and guidance of his superiors in his presentations. As a result, he noticed that his colleagues became more open, more receptive, and even more trusting of his ideas.

A simple but powerful way to show humility is through your language. Adding phrases like "with your guidance" or "thanks to your support" can subtly reinforce your respect for authority. Japanese colleagues notice these details, and a little humility goes a long way in ensuring you're seen as a respectful team player rather than an ambitious outsider.

# Learning to Read the Atmosphere

JAPANESE WORKPLACES place a high value on *kūki wo yomu*—literally, "reading the air." It's a skill that involves sensing the mood and unspoken expectations in a room. Knowing when to speak and when to hold back is an art form, one that relies on observing cues that are often subtle. If you want to fit in, developing this skill is essential, as it helps you understand when it's appropriate to contribute and when it's best to support.

One experience that stands out involved a team meeting where I'd planned to propose a minor shift in project direction. As the discussion unfolded, though, I noticed that the mood was tense, with several colleagues visibly uncomfortable about the project's timeline. Sensing the atmosphere, I decided against introducing my idea right then. Instead, I waited until a later date when the mood was lighter, and my suggestion was received far more openly.

Learning to read the atmosphere isn't easy, especially if you're not used to relying on non-verbal cues. But over time, paying attention to the subtleties—like body language, the tone of a meeting, and even the amount of eye contact—helps you gauge when it's appropriate to share your thoughts. Japanese colleagues respect those who understand these unspoken rules and show patience by waiting for the right moment.

## Earning the Right to Contribute

RESPECTING AUTHORITY doesn't mean surrendering your input altogether. In fact, once you've earned your place in the hierarchy, your contributions will be valued more deeply. Building trust takes time in Japan, but once it's established, your voice will carry weight. In my experience, the key to fitting in is to respect the process: prove your dedication, show your humility, and contribute when appropriate.

Over time, you'll find that senior colleagues begin to invite your perspective, and your role shifts from a quiet observer to a trusted contributor. It's a gradual process, but it's one that brings rewards. Japanese colleagues, once they trust you, appreciate your expertise and insight. By showing respect for the established structure, you earn the right to influence it. The paradox is that in respecting authority, you eventually gain it.

Fitting into a Japanese workplace requires a shift in mindset. It's not about pushing your ideas through; it's about respecting the values that underpin the organisation and finding a way to work within them. In Japan, the workplace is more than a job—it's a community. And respecting authority isn't a limitation; it's a pathway to belonging, understanding, and eventually, genuine influence.

# Chapter 9: Common Complaints – Hypocrisy, Overwork, and Cold Formality

Japan's workplace culture, while admired for its discipline and order, has its fair share of drawbacks. Beneath the veneer of politeness and harmony, there exists a side to Japanese corporate life that can feel stifling, even oppressive. Many of these challenges are rooted in the emphasis on formality, hierarchical respect, and the seemingly relentless drive to maintain *wa* (harmony) at all costs. For all its strengths, the Japanese workplace can sometimes feel like a double-edged sword.

For those who join Japanese firms with hopes of collaborative, fulfilling work, the realities of this environment can feel isolating. The combination of overwork, strict formality, and the expectation to "keep up appearances" often creates a strained atmosphere. It's an open secret that many Japanese employees are drained by the daily grind, but the culture's resistance to change keeps these frustrations locked beneath a polite exterior. Here are some of the most pervasive complaints that workers face, issues that are often masked by formalities but deeply embedded in the corporate structure.

## The Surface-Level Harmony and Its Underlying Hypocrisy

JAPANESE WORKPLACES place a strong emphasis on maintaining harmony, but there's an unspoken hypocrisy that comes with it. While everyone is polite and formal on the surface, true feelings and honest opinions are rarely expressed openly. This approach creates a kind of "faux harmony," where issues are acknowledged privately but never addressed head-on, allowing problems to fester without resolution. For employees, this creates a workplace dynamic that can feel insincere and stifling. People go through the motions of teamwork without actually working as a cohesive team.

A colleague once confided in me that her team had been struggling with a project for months because no one wanted to voice their concerns directly. The project manager, who was clearly overwhelmed, continued to issue vague instructions, hoping the team would somehow "understand" what was needed. The team members, in turn, pretended to be on board, only to silently pass on their frustrations in private conversations. No one wanted to break the harmony by acknowledging the elephant in the room—that the project was off track and the manager was out of his depth. This performative agreement is all too common and leads to an atmosphere where everyone is "agreeing" without actually agreeing on anything substantial.

For those of us accustomed to transparent communication, this insincere agreement can feel like a betrayal of basic teamwork principles. Decisions that should be debated are instead handled with polite nods, leaving misunderstandings to accumulate. In many cases, this "face-saving" facade leads to rework, wasted resources, and a loss of morale. Employees feel that they're tiptoeing around issues rather than solving them, fostering a sense of alienation from their work. Over time, it's a hypocrisy that wears people down, draining motivation and leading to burnout.

## Overwork and the Culture of Karoshi

JAPAN IS NOTORIOUS for its culture of overwork, so much so that it has a term for death by overwork: *karoshi*. The expectation to work long hours is deeply ingrained, and while unpaid overtime has technically been regulated, the unspoken pressure to stay late remains. Many Japanese employees feel obligated to stay as long as their manager, creating a chain reaction that keeps everyone in the office long past regular hours. The unfortunate reality is that staying late isn't always about productivity—it's often about demonstrating loyalty to the company.

The concept of *service overtime*, where employees work extra hours without additional pay, is common, despite official company policies against it. Employees stay late to show dedication, not necessarily because they're being efficient or accomplishing more. This culture of overwork is particularly tough on younger employees, who enter the workforce with the expectation that these long hours are part of "paying their dues." It's a culture that prioritises presence over productivity, where time spent at the desk is often valued over the quality of work produced.

One of my Japanese colleagues once admitted to me, in a rare moment of candour, that he spent a lot of his "overtime" simply trying to look busy. "It's not about working harder," he said, "it's about showing that you're here." For many, this performative workday creates a draining cycle. Employees are exhausted, but they continue to stay late because leaving before their manager would be seen as disrespectful. This ritualistic dedication often pushes people to their limits, and it's a practice that's hard to break—especially in a culture where job security and loyalty are prized above all else.

The toll on mental health is significant. Many employees feel trapped, balancing their dedication to the company with the wear and tear on their personal lives. It's common to hear stories of employees developing stress-related illnesses or suffering from burnout, all while maintaining a stoic exterior. In some cases, the pressure becomes so intense that employees suffer breakdowns, or worse, become casualties of *karoshi*. It's a tragic outcome of a work culture that places duty to the company above duty to oneself, an expectation that's almost impossible to question without risking alienation.

## The Cold Formality: Professional but Distant

JAPANESE OFFICE CULTURE is formal, and this formality often comes at the expense of warmth and genuine connection. Employees maintain a professional distance, and it's rare for people to share personal thoughts or form close friendships at work. This coolness can feel isolating, especially for anyone who values camaraderie in the workplace. Meetings are structured, feedback is given in reserved language, and most interactions remain strictly business. While this creates an efficient environment, it also prevents employees from building meaningful connections with each other.

For foreign employees, the cold formality can be one of the hardest aspects to adjust to. There's no chitchat by the coffee machine, no shared jokes during a team lunch. It's as if everyone has a wall up, and breaking through it takes patience and perseverance. I've seen colleagues who tried to foster a more open atmosphere, only to find their efforts subtly rebuffed. In many cases, Japanese employees simply aren't comfortable with blending personal and professional lives, seeing the workplace as a domain solely for work.

Nancy once tried to organise a team outing as a way to build rapport, a common practice in the West. But the response was lukewarm at best; colleagues politely declined or joined out of obligation rather than genuine enthusiasm. She soon learned that in Japan, social interactions are typically saved for carefully structured events, like the *nomikai*, rather than spontaneous outings. The formality isn't necessarily a lack of friendliness—it's simply a boundary that Japanese workers maintain to keep work and personal life separate. But this boundary often leaves the office atmosphere feeling cold and impersonal, with employees operating more like cogs in a machine than as members of a cohesive team.

Over time, this distance erodes morale. Without a sense of connection or belonging, employees often feel like they're just fulfilling a role rather than contributing to a shared mission. For those of us who are used to building bonds at work, the Japanese office can feel strangely hollow. This cool professionalism may keep the office functioning smoothly, but it's a sterile atmosphere that leaves many longing for a bit of genuine human warmth.

In the Japanese workplace, these cultural challenges—surface-level harmony, the expectation of overwork, and the cold formality—combine to create an environment that can be daunting. While Japanese employees often take these norms in stride, for those who come from cultures that value open communication and personal connection, it can feel like trying to work with one hand tied behind your back. These complaints aren't just superficial; they point to fundamental issues within Japanese corporate culture that, left unaddressed, can make the workplace feel more like a gauntlet than a community. And for those who push against these norms, there are even more extreme consequences, which we'll delve into in the next chapter.

# Chapter 10: Extreme Cases – Johnny Kitagawa and Train Suicides: When Pressure Goes Too Far

In Japanese society, workplace pressures can extend to tragic extremes. The same forces that demand harmony and loyalty can, at times, create an environment so suffocating that people feel trapped, with no way out. Two powerful examples illustrate this reality: the decades-long abuse allegations surrounding entertainment mogul Johnny Kitagawa and the devastatingly common phenomenon of train suicides. These are stark reminders of how Japan's focus on respect, hierarchy, and unyielding dedication can, if left unchecked, push people beyond their limits.

## The Dark Legacy of Johnny Kitagawa: Power and Exploitation in the Workplace

THE CASE OF JOHNNY Kitagawa, founder of Johnny & Associates, Japan's most prominent talent agency, is one of the most notorious examples of unchecked power and workplace exploitation in modern Japan. For decades, Kitagawa was accused of sexually abusing young male talents under his management—yet for most of his life, these accusations went largely ignored. The Japanese media and entertainment industry, bound by implicit respect for his status and authority, were reluctant to expose his actions. He wielded immense power, and those around him were complicit, either out of fear or a desire to protect their own interests.

Kitagawa's influence in Japan's entertainment industry was so extensive that many felt speaking out was impossible. Employees, former talents, and even journalists avoided addressing the abuse allegations due to the fear of being blacklisted. The concept of *enryo*—the Japanese tendency to hold back or refrain from overstepping—played a major role. People respected Kitagawa's authority and didn't dare question him publicly. The case is a grim example of how, when respect for hierarchy goes unchallenged, it can become a breeding ground for abuse.

It wasn't until after his death in 2019 that the allegations finally came to light in a significant way. For years, Kitagawa's influence had been so dominant that the Japanese media, even when aware of his actions, kept silent. The lack of accountability allowed him to operate without restraint, exploiting his power in a way that would be unthinkable in many other cultures. It was a painful reminder that authority, when combined with an unwillingness to disrupt the status quo, can create conditions where abuse festers.

The Kitagawa scandal forces Japan to confront the cultural factors that allowed it to happen: a reluctance to question authority, an unspoken rule against breaking harmony, and a society that sometimes prioritises appearances over justice. It's a brutal example of what can happen when respect for hierarchy overshadows basic human rights. For Japanese society, the case remains a wake-up call—highlighting the need for accountability in workplaces and a more open discourse about abuse of power.

## The Grim Reality of Train Suicides: When Work Culture Turns Deadly

WHILE JOHNNY KITAGAWA'S case speaks to the dangers of unchecked power, the phenomenon of train suicides in Japan represents the darker side of societal pressure. Train suicides are so frequent that rail companies have developed protocols to handle them efficiently, minimising delays and even apologising for the disruption. Yet behind these statistics lie stories of people driven to their limits by a relentless work culture that demands absolute dedication, often at the expense of mental health.

In Japan, suicide is not only a personal tragedy but also a societal burden, one that starkly reveals the intense pressures of conformity and loyalty. Many of these suicides occur during rush hours, when individuals heading to or from work are overcome by the despair of enduring yet another day in an environment where they feel unseen and unsupported. The problem is so common that train platforms in Tokyo and other major cities have installed barriers to prevent people from jumping onto the tracks.

These tragedies are, in many cases, the direct result of overwork, isolation, and the inability to openly address personal struggles. In Japanese work culture, there is often an unspoken expectation to "endure" without complaint, and mental health issues are rarely discussed openly. Even within companies, there's a reluctance to offer support or flexibility for employees dealing with stress. The concept of *gaman*, or enduring hardship, is deeply ingrained, and many employees internalise the idea that they must bear their burdens alone, without disrupting the group.

One of the most tragic aspects of train suicides is the lack of public dialogue around mental health. While companies have begun to acknowledge the impact of overwork, mental health remains a largely taboo topic. Employees who struggle with depression or anxiety may feel too ashamed to seek help, fearing they'll be viewed as weak or unreliable. Instead, they push on, suppressing their emotions, until the weight becomes unbearable.

The societal impact is also striking: families are sometimes held financially accountable for the "inconvenience" caused by their loved ones' suicides, with rail companies charging them for the disruption.

This adds another layer of shame and financial hardship, deterring open discussions about mental health and reinforcing the stigma around seeking help. The result is a tragic cycle where individuals facing immense pressure see no viable solution, and the system remains largely indifferent to their suffering.

## Learning from These Extremes: A Need for Change in Corporate and Societal Mindsets

JOHNNY KITAGAWA'S LEGACY and the issue of train suicides underscore a critical need for Japan to address the darker aspects of its workplace culture. There's an increasing call for change, but progress remains slow. To prevent future abuses and tragedies, Japanese workplaces need to develop environments where authority is balanced with accountability, and where mental health is recognised as a legitimate concern.

For too long, respect for authority has been treated as an unassailable rule in Japanese workplaces, but the Kitagawa case shows that unchecked power can lead to devastating consequences. The reluctance to question authority needs to be replaced with a healthy level of accountability—employees should feel empowered to speak up when something feels wrong, without fearing retaliation or ostracism. In recent years, some companies have begun implementing internal reporting systems, but these are still rare, and trust in such systems is limited.

The issue of train suicides highlights another pressing need: a shift in attitudes towards work-life balance and mental health. Companies are starting to introduce reforms, such as encouraging employees to leave on time and offering counselling services. However, these changes are often met with scepticism, as they clash with long-standing cultural expectations of dedication and endurance. For real change to occur, there needs to be a societal shift towards accepting vulnerability, recognising that mental health is as essential as physical health.

In the face of these extreme examples, Japanese society is beginning to grapple with the darker consequences of its traditional values. While the respect for hierarchy, dedication to work, and commitment to harmony are qualities that have contributed to Japan's success, there's also a growing understanding that these values need to evolve. The next step for Japan's workplaces is to find a balance—one where respect doesn't equate to blind obedience, and where harmony includes space for open dialogue and mental well-being.

# Part 4: The Post-COVID Changes to the Japanese Workplace

# Chapter 11: Foreign Funds and New Cultural Currents in Japanese Corporations

In recent years, Japan's economy has seen a surge of foreign investment, as overseas funds eye opportunities in Japan's stable, yet aging market. It's an interesting shift—one that's slowly reshaping the landscape of Japanese business culture, much to the apprehension of traditional corporate leaders. The infusion of foreign funds, particularly from North American and European companies, is challenging long-standing norms, injecting fresh perspectives and, to the dismay of some Japanese executives, a more open, international ethos into the workplace.

Just the other night, my wife asked me what I thought about the news of a Canadian company buying a significant stake in Japan's iconic 7-Eleven. "Isn't that a bit unsettling?" she asked, echoing the sentiments of Japanese commentators worried about foreign influence. I shrugged, perhaps a bit dismissively. "It's about time," I replied. For years, Japan's corporate culture has been insular, deeply protective of its traditions, and frankly, resistant to change. With foreign funds coming in, there's an opportunity to bring a bit of American dynamism into the mix.

# The Influence of Foreign Acquisitions on Japanese Corporate Culture

ONE OF THE MOST HIGH-profile recent deals involved Canada's Seven & i Holdings acquiring a larger stake in the Japanese 7-Eleven franchise, which dominates convenience store culture across Japan. This deal, while financially sound, has raised concerns among Japanese corporate leaders, who fear that foreign influence could erode the brand's "Japanese-ness" and reshape the very foundation of their workplace culture. And it's not just 7-Eleven—other foreign investors are also buying stakes in established Japanese brands, from retail giants to tech companies.

A few of my friends—executives from U.S. firms who have long been doing business in Japan—found the backlash a bit humorous. One of them quipped over dinner, "If anything, Japan could use a bit of a shake-up." There's a perception that injecting American-style innovation and efficiency might benefit Japan's corporate world, where decision-making can be painstakingly slow, and hierarchy often stifles creativity. Another friend chimed in, noting that Japanese companies have remained globally competitive for years but could stand to loosen up, adopt a bit more of the agile, quick-to-adapt mindset that's second nature in American firms.

Japanese executives, however, are wary. Some worry that foreign-owned firms will undermine Japan's revered work ethic, that employees might grow too "individualistic" or prioritize personal life over duty to the company. It's a sentiment rooted in a long-standing fear of cultural erosion, and one that hints at a deeper anxiety within Japan's business community. After all, Japanese corporations have traditionally valued harmony, conformity, and dedication to the group—values that might clash with the relatively more relaxed, work-life balance-focused cultures of Western countries.

Yet, the writing is on the wall. With Japan's demographic crisis worsening and a shortage of skilled labour, foreign investment may not be just beneficial; it may be necessary. American, Canadian, and European funds bring not only capital but also managerial expertise and operational strategies that could help Japanese companies streamline their operations. For instance, foreign-led firms are often quicker to implement productivity-enhancing tools, data-driven decision-making, and a more casual approach to hierarchy—elements that Japan's traditional corporate culture has been slow to adopt.

## Dismissing the "Paranoia" Around Foreign Influence

TO MANY IN THE INTERNATIONAL business community, these fears seem overblown. Foreign investments bring fresh opportunities for growth and efficiency. The way I see it, these cultural changes aren't a threat—they're a step forward. Injecting American funds and ideas into Japanese companies won't lead to a complete cultural overhaul. Instead, it could offer a pragmatic blend of old and new, where Japan's strengths are retained, but adapted to the demands of a modern economy.

When my wife mentioned another news segment showing interviews with CEOs who were wary of "Western influence" taking over, I chuckled. "It's ironic," I told her, "Japan's own companies have been investing in the U.S. for decades without any qualms." Japanese corporations like Sony, Toyota, and SoftBank have had a massive presence in global markets for years, buying up tech firms, real estate, and even American entertainment companies. Why, then, the reluctance to welcome foreign investments back home?

One of my colleagues, Paul, who's worked in Japan for nearly two decades, agrees that Japanese leaders' fears are more paranoia than valid concerns. "If anything," he argues, "foreign funds force Japanese companies to rethink their inefficiencies." The injection of outside capital pressures companies to adopt more transparent governance practices and shed the layers of unnecessary bureaucracy that have often slowed down Japanese decision-making processes. Foreign investors tend to push for greater accountability, clarity in communication, and, yes, even shorter work hours. These aren't threats—they're tools that can help Japan adapt to a rapidly changing world.

The view within Japan's younger workforce is also telling. Many younger employees, especially those who have studied or worked abroad, see foreign influence as a welcome change. They're hungry for a workplace that values efficiency, merit, and work-life balance—a place where they can feel fulfilled without sacrificing their well-being. One young analyst I know shared with me that, in his opinion, "It's refreshing to see foreigners bring new ideas here. It gives us hope that change is possible." To him, foreign funds represent more than just capital; they symbolize a shift towards a more balanced and forward-thinking work environment.

As foreign acquisitions continue to rise, Japan's corporate leaders may eventually have to adapt, whether they like it or not. The global marketplace won't wait for tradition to catch up. Western funds will continue to bring new cultural influences into Japanese boardrooms, and companies will need to find ways to integrate these without compromising their identity. But instead of viewing it as a threat, Japan's corporations could see it as an opportunity to retain what makes them unique while evolving to stay competitive on the world stage.

In the end, dismissing foreign influence as merely an erosion of Japanese values overlooks the benefits that come with it. For a country known for its adaptability and resilience, the injection of Western funds and ideas could represent the next logical step in Japan's corporate evolution. As my friends and I often say, "A bit of American pragmatism won't hurt." After all, if Japanese companies can embrace change overseas, there's no reason they can't do the same at home.

# Chapter 12: The New Face of Japanese Workplace Culture – Post-COVID Changes Amid Labor Shortages

As Japan grapples with a serious labor shortage, companies have had to adapt quickly. With one of the oldest populations in the world, Japan's workforce is shrinking, forcing both businesses and policymakers to rethink traditional approaches. The year 2024 has marked a turning point, with corporations rolling out changes aimed at improving work-life balance, offering more flexible hours, and embracing remote work options. These shifts, while slow in coming, represent a new chapter in Japan's corporate landscape—one driven by necessity rather than choice.

My wife recently asked me what I thought of all these reforms, and frankly, it feels long overdue. "Japan has always been known for its relentless work culture," she pointed out, "so what changed?" The answer, I told her, is a blend of demographic pressures and the need to compete globally. In the past, Japanese companies could rely on a steady flow of dedicated employees, but now, with fewer workers and an aging population, companies have no choice but to adapt. My friends in the industry agree; it's no longer just about preserving tradition—it's about survival.

# Flexible Work Hours and Remote Work as a New Norm

ONE OF THE BIGGEST changes has been the shift toward flexible work hours. For years, Japan's office culture was synonymous with long hours and fixed schedules, but in 2024, companies are increasingly offering options like staggered start times and even four-day workweeks. The traditional "salaryman" image—employees in identical suits, commuting to work every day—feels a bit outdated as companies try to attract and retain talent.

The pandemic accelerated this shift toward flexibility, and now, with labor shortages mounting, companies have made it official. Many corporations are allowing employees to choose when they start and end their days, provided they complete their tasks. This shift is especially appealing to younger workers, who crave more control over their schedules and work-life balance. A colleague of mine who oversees operations at a tech firm in Osaka told me, "We'd never have considered remote work a few years ago, but now, it's practically a requirement." According to him, allowing flexibility has helped his company attract talent that would have otherwise left for more progressive employers.

Remote work, once seen as a temporary pandemic solution, has also gained traction as a permanent option. Japanese companies are increasingly setting up infrastructure to support employees working from home, with major firms like Fujitsu and Hitachi adopting hybrid models. One of my friends, who works in management at a Tokyo-based software company, shared how his firm invested heavily in remote work tools this year to meet demand. "It's not just about convenience," he told me. "It's a way to keep employees engaged and happy, especially when we can't fill every role as easily as we used to."

# Enhanced Work-Life Balance Initiatives and

# Mental Health Support

JAPAN'S NOTORIOUS "WORK till you drop" culture has also softened in recent years, and 2024 marks a big step forward in promoting work-life balance. With a dwindling labor force, companies are realising that it's not sustainable to push employees to their limits. Instead, they're prioritising measures that encourage productivity while respecting personal time. Companies like Toyota and Shiseido have been offering paid leave incentives, encouraging employees to actually use their vacation days, a concept that was once foreign to many Japanese workers.

Another significant shift is the growing focus on mental health support. For years, discussing mental health was considered taboo in Japanese offices, but as the conversation around work-life balance becomes more mainstream, companies are starting to address it directly. More firms are offering access to counselling services, encouraging regular mental health check-ins, and implementing stress management workshops. I remember talking with a Japanese HR executive last year who mentioned that these changes have been crucial in retaining talent, particularly among younger employees who are more open about prioritising mental health.

My friend Nancy, who has worked in Japan for over a decade, said she's noticed a real shift in her colleagues' attitudes. "It used to be a badge of honour to work through stress, but now, companies are telling people to take time for themselves." She recently saw her firm introduce "wellness days" that allow employees to take a day off with no questions asked, a policy that would have been unimaginable a few years ago. For employees, these changes signal a new corporate culture that values individuals' well-being as much as their output—a fundamental shift in how work is perceived in Japan.

# Automation and AI: Filling the Labor Gaps

WITH FEWER WORKERS available, automation has become a cornerstone of Japanese companies' strategy to maintain productivity. In 2024, we're seeing even more investment in AI and robotics, from manufacturing to customer service. Companies like Panasonic and Toyota have been pioneers in adopting automation, not only to streamline processes but to make up for the lack of human resources. This increased reliance on technology has also transformed the workplace, as employees are now required to work alongside AI systems and learn new skills to operate and manage automated workflows.

A colleague who works in the automotive industry shared how his plant recently integrated AI-driven quality control systems. "It's almost like the robots have become part of the team," he joked, but he noted that this integration of AI has been crucial in keeping production levels high despite a smaller workforce. Automation allows employees to focus on higher-value tasks, and it's slowly redefining job roles, creating a more collaborative space between humans and machines.

However, this shift towards automation isn't universally accepted. Traditionalists within companies still view it with suspicion, fearing that increased reliance on machines will dilute the personal touch that Japanese companies are known for. But with the workforce shrinking, AI and robotics are becoming essential rather than optional. As one executive put it, "We have to choose between embracing technology or facing constant understaffing."

# Diversity and Inclusion Efforts: Tapping into Untapped Resources

THE LABOR SHORTAGE has also prompted companies to tap into previously overlooked segments of the workforce, such as women, the elderly, and foreign workers. In 2024, Japanese companies are implementing more inclusive hiring practices to create a more diverse workforce. Many firms are pushing for more female participation, a significant change in a country where gender roles have traditionally been rigid.

Companies like SoftBank and Uniqlo are making strides to recruit older workers, offering roles that accommodate physical limitations and flexible hours. Even foreign workers, once a rarity in many Japanese companies, are now seen as essential contributors. With immigration policies gradually relaxing, Japanese firms are opening their doors to skilled foreign workers, bringing a new dynamic to the workplace.

It's a necessary adjustment, and one that companies hope will help balance the labor deficit. My friend Paul, who manages a team of both Japanese and foreign employees, shared that he's seen a positive shift in workplace dynamics. "Having different backgrounds brings new ideas to the table," he said, "and it's actually helping us tackle old problems with fresh perspectives." Japan's slowly changing attitude towards diversity in the workplace reflects a pragmatic approach to the labor crisis—one that will hopefully make workplaces not only more inclusive but also more resilient in the long run.

In 2024, Japan's corporate reforms represent a pragmatic response to the pressures of an aging and shrinking workforce. By prioritising flexibility, work-life balance, mental health, and technology, companies are attempting to create a more sustainable work environment, one that appeals to both younger employees and international talent. These changes, while driven by necessity, are reshaping Japan's corporate culture in ways that seemed impossible just a few years ago.

For companies to thrive in the years ahead, adapting to these new realities isn't optional—it's essential. Japan's labor shortage has pushed corporations to reconsider what it means to work, encouraging a more humane, flexible, and inclusive approach that could redefine Japanese work culture for generations to come.

# Chapter 13: The New Generation of Japanese Entrepreneurs and Evolving Work Styles

In recent years, Japan has witnessed a significant shift in its work culture, driven by a new generation of entrepreneurs and a workforce that values flexibility and autonomy over traditional employment models. This transformation is reshaping the Japanese business landscape, offering alternative career paths such as part-time work, freelancing, and employment under progressive business owners. However, despite these changes, the core principles of Japanese workplace etiquette remain deeply ingrained, especially in companies led by Japanese management.

## Emergence of Young Entrepreneurs and Flexible Work Models

THE RISE OF YOUNG JAPANESE entrepreneurs has introduced innovative business models that prioritize employee well-being and work-life balance. These leaders are challenging the conventional norms of lifelong employment and hierarchical structures, offering more flexible work arrangements. For instance, some startups are implementing shorter workweeks and remote work options to attract and retain talent.

My friend's son, Donald, recently sought my advice on navigating this evolving business environment. He shared an anecdote about his hairstylist in Harajuku, who had changed salons four times over two years, even venturing into freelancing before returning to employment. This hairstylist's journey reflects a broader trend among young professionals seeking environments that align with their personal and professional aspirations.

## The Freelance Economy and Part-Time Work

THE FREELANCE ECONOMY in Japan has experienced significant growth, with more professionals opting for independent work arrangements. This trend, driven by a desire for greater flexibility and autonomy, is expected to continue. Between 2015 and 2021, Japan's freelance population grew by 68.3%, reaching 6.4 million people by 2021. During the same period, the freelance economy in Japan expanded by 62.7%, amounting to 9.2 trillion Japanese Yen.

Additionally, many young Japanese are choosing part-time positions that offer shorter hours, allowing them to pursue personal interests or multiple income streams. This shift indicates a departure from the traditional expectation of long working hours and a single career path.

## Cultural Adaptation in Diverse Work Environments

AS BUSINESSES WORK models and diverse working styles, the core principles of Japanese business culture—like *wa* (harmony), *enryo*(restraint), and *giri* (duty or obligation)—still hold considerable weight. Younger company owners are aware that deviating too far from these values may alienate some employees or clients who value tradition. So, while there's room for creative freedom and a push for balance, many of these companies still retain a foundation rooted in Japanese cultural norms.

This fusion of new thinking and traditional values creates a unique work environment where flexibility is encouraged, but courtesy, respect, and hierarchy are never fully abandoned. In Donald's case, his hairstylist may find more autonomy in a foreigner-dominated salon, but if he moves to a Japanese-owned salon, the expectation for traditional workplace decorum returns. It's as though a delicate dance has emerged in these new companies, where employees are given freedom, yet are gently reminded to align with Japanese values whenever necessary.

### How Young Professionals Are Navigating the New Landscape

The younger Japanese workforce is increasingly selective, gravitating towards companies or positions that offer meaningful work-life balance and alignment with their personal goals. Freelancers, part-timers, and those working in start-ups are shaping their careers with an openness that their parents' generation rarely had. Many of them, like Donald's hairstylist, don't hesitate to change jobs if they find an opportunity that better fits their lifestyle or personal preferences. This adaptability is becoming a hallmark of the new generation, creating a dynamic in the workplace that's much more fluid than the rigid structure of traditional Japanese employment.

For instance, a friend's daughter recently transitioned from a corporate job in finance to a freelance consulting role. She said, "I feel more in control of my life this way. I can choose my clients, set my own hours, and take breaks when I need them." Her sentiments are echoed by many young Japanese professionals who view freelancing not as a fallback but as a preferred way of working. This flexibility is increasingly attractive in a country where loyalty to a single company is no longer a given and where career paths are far from linear.

### The Role of Social Media in Shaping Modern Japanese Business Culture

Another interesting factor in this shift is the influence of social media. Young professionals in Japan are watching trends worldwide, where people share insights into flexible work models, remote working success stories, and the importance of mental well-being. They see their counterparts in countries like the U.S., Canada, and Europe enjoying a balanced work-life approach, and many are inspired to seek the same in Japan. Platforms like Instagram and LinkedIn have become channels where Japanese professionals connect with global trends, fostering a mindset shift that embraces individual needs over corporate loyalty.

In a recent conversation with Paul, who's been observing these trends from his own business in Tokyo, he mentioned how younger Japanese employees are increasingly vocal about what they want in the workplace. "It's as if social media has given them permission to ask for things that were once unthinkable here," he said. "They're asking for shorter hours, remote work, and more job satisfaction." This cultural shift, spurred on by global influences, is gradually making Japanese workplaces more adaptable and responsive to individual needs.

### The Challenges Ahead: Reconciling Change with Tradition

Despite these progressive steps, Japan's new wave of entrepreneurs and workers face the challenge of integrating flexible work models without completely upending traditional values. There is still a strong emphasis on respect for authority, punctuality, and group harmony, especially in businesses where older, more traditional leaders are in place. In these companies, younger workers are expected to "play by the rules" and adjust to a slower pace of change.

Many young Japanese are finding themselves in environments where they can embrace a more modern approach to work but must still adhere to certain cultural norms. Donald's hairstylist, for example, may enjoy the variety and freedom of freelancing and switching salons but would still need to show the same level of courtesy and respect to Japanese management if he joins a traditional company. It's a constant balancing act for those straddling these two worlds.

In the end, while Japan's work culture is evolving, it's not a full departure from its roots. For companies to thrive and attract young talent, they need to create workplaces that accommodate modern work preferences while respecting the enduring values of Japanese society.

The new generation of Japanese entrepreneurs understands that blending flexibility with tradition is the best way forward, creating a work environment that's progressive yet distinctly Japanese. And perhaps, with time, this balance will allow Japan to retain the essence of its corporate culture while adapting to a more modern, globalised world.

# Part 5: Strategies for Successfully Navigating Japanese Work Culture

# Chapter 14: Step Back and Analyse – Is This a 'Respect' Issue or Pure Formality?

**1. Observe Reactions, Not Just Actions**

In Japanese culture, actions are sometimes more symbolic than sincere. Instead of focusing solely on what's being done, observe people's reactions. For example, if you bow upon entering a meeting and your colleagues don't bow as deeply in return, it may signal that your formality wasn't expected or was more than necessary. If they return the bow deeply and with attention, however, you'll know your gesture hit the mark.

**Tip:** When in doubt, mirror the behaviour of those around you, especially in new settings. Watch for subtleties like how long they maintain eye contact, how formal their language is, or the depth of their bow, and adapt accordingly.

**2. Read Body Language and Tone for Cues on Hierarchy**

Hierarchy is ever-present in Japanese workplaces, but not every senior employee expects the same level of deference. Some leaders prefer an informal approach despite their status, while others strictly observe protocol. Before assuming you need to be overly deferential, look for signs in their body language and tone. If a senior manager engages casually or encourages open discussion, you're likely in an environment that values practicality over strict formality.

**Tip:** Pay attention to how others speak to this person and imitate that tone. If you're unsure, opt for a respectful approach but dial it down if you notice a more relaxed vibe. You can always adjust based on their reactions to your tone and gestures.

### 3. Practice the "Polite Pause" Before Offering Opinions

When engaging in discussions, especially with senior team members, make it a habit to pause briefly before responding or sharing your opinions. In Japan, taking a moment to think before you speak is a subtle way of showing that you're carefully considering what was said—an unspoken form of respect. This practice signals that you're not rushing to respond, which can sometimes come across as overly assertive or even disrespectful.

**Tip**: A few seconds of silence before you reply can convey humility and thoughtfulness, qualities highly valued in Japan. Practice this "polite pause" to avoid appearing too eager or blunt, especially in formal meetings.

### 4. Use Conditional Phrasing to Test Boundaries

If you need to suggest a change or express a differing opinion, start with conditional phrasing rather than direct language. Phrases like "Perhaps we could consider..." or "I wonder if it might be helpful to..." convey openness without undermining authority. This approach allows you to gauge how receptive people are to your ideas without overstepping. In Japan, soft language is often a way to introduce new ideas while maintaining harmony.

**Tip**: Always frame suggestions as possibilities rather than directives. This helps you test how firm the boundaries are while showing deference to existing practices.

### 5. Adopt Formal Titles and Gradually Adjust

In Western workplaces, using first names can build rapport quickly, but in Japan, titles often signal respect. If you're unsure how formal you need to be, start with titles (like "-san" or "Manager Tanaka") and observe whether others around you switch to first names. Over time, your colleagues may invite you to address them informally, but this should come from them rather than you taking the initiative.

**Tip**: When first introduced, always use formal titles and honorifics. Gradually adjust based on the cues you receive, especially if your colleagues switch to first names themselves.

### 6. Pay Attention to the "Overly Agreeable" Responses

If your ideas or suggestions are met with an enthusiastic "yes" or "I see," pay close attention to the tone and body language accompanying it. In Japan, agreeing outright doesn't always mean genuine approval. Often, overly polite responses are a way of saving face or avoiding open confrontation. A truly supportive response will typically involve specific follow-up questions or an active engagement with your proposal.

**Tip**: If you receive a positive response that feels a bit too polished, it's wise to follow up. Ask, "Do you think there's anything that could improve this?" or "Are there any other considerations we should keep in mind?" This allows your colleague to express reservations more comfortably.

### 7. Ask for Feedback One-on-One When Unsure

In a group setting, Japanese colleagues might hesitate to give you direct feedback to avoid disrupting harmony. If you're uncertain about how well your contributions are being received, approach a trusted colleague one-on-one to ask for feedback. Private settings allow for more candid responses and help you gauge whether you're navigating formalities correctly.

**Tip**: Ask, "Do you think I'm following the right approach here?" or "Is there anything I could adjust in my communication style?" This way, you show willingness to improve without putting anyone on the spot publicly.

### 8. Use Self-Deprecation to Show Humility

Japanese culture places high value on humility, so a little self-deprecation can go a long way in showing respect. When you present an idea or share an achievement, it's often more respectful to downplay it slightly, allowing your colleagues or superiors to decide its merit. This approach avoids seeming overly confident, which can sometimes be seen as lacking humility.

**Tip**: When sharing an idea, preface it with, "This might not be the best approach, but I thought I'd share…" or "I'm still learning, so please let me know if there's a better way." This way, you invite constructive feedback rather than positioning yourself as an authority.

### 9. Observe Senior Colleagues' Boundaries Around Formality

Not every Japanese workplace expects the same level of formal ritual. Senior colleagues can provide a good indication of the boundaries. In some teams, you might find that even senior managers appreciate a more informal approach as long as you're competent. Conversely, some companies maintain a strict adherence to hierarchy regardless of role. Observing these subtle cues can help you determine how much formality is truly required.

**Tip**: Ask a senior colleague if there are specific practices to follow or areas where formality is expected. Most colleagues will appreciate your thoughtfulness and guide you on how best to approach interactions.

By practicing these strategies, you'll not only learn to distinguish between genuine respect and procedural formalities, but you'll also develop a more intuitive sense of when to observe tradition and when to relax. The aim is to keep the peace without overextending yourself, striking a balance between fitting in and maintaining authenticity. With these practical tools, you can navigate Japanese workplace culture more confidently, avoiding common pitfalls and building respectful, effective relationships.

# Chapter 15: Understanding Japanese Efficiency – Robots, AI, and Saving Costs

Japanese businesses have long been known for their efficiency and precision, but in recent years, these qualities have been amplified by a strong emphasis on technology. As Japan faces a declining population and labour shortages, companies are turning to robots, AI, and automation to streamline operations and maintain productivity. For anyone working in Japan, understanding how these technologies are integrated into daily workflows—and learning how to adapt to them—is essential for success. This chapter provides practical tips for navigating the high-tech side of Japanese workplaces and using it to your advantage.

## Embrace the Automation Mindset

IN JAPANESE WORKPLACES, automation is more than just a trend; it's a necessity. From automated customer service kiosks in retail stores to robotic arms in factories, companies rely on technology to fill gaps in the workforce. The key here isn't just to be comfortable with technology but to see it as an integral part of your role. Many Japanese companies expect employees to work alongside robots and AI systems, not only to speed up processes but also to reduce human error.

**Tip:** Familiarise yourself with the specific technologies used in your workplace. If your company uses AI tools for scheduling or robotic systems on the production floor, take the time to understand their functions. This familiarity will allow you to adapt faster and communicate more effectively with both your human and "robotic" colleagues.

## Leverage AI to Enhance Efficiency

IN SOME COMPANIES, AI is integrated into everyday tasks, such as scheduling, data analysis, and even decision-making. Japan's approach to AI isn't just about replacing tasks; it's about enhancing accuracy and productivity. For instance, many firms use AI to optimise supply chains, predict maintenance needs, or monitor project timelines. This allows employees to focus on high-value tasks rather than getting bogged down in routine work.

**Tip**: Use AI to your advantage. If your company offers training on AI tools or suggests best practices, take these seriously. Consider AI not as a replacement but as a productivity partner. Familiarising yourself with how AI can support your daily responsibilities will make your workday smoother and show that you're proactive about adapting to Japan's tech-forward environment.

## Adapt to Streamlined Processes Without Losing Your Personal Touch

WHILE EFFICIENCY IS critical, Japanese workplaces still value the human element, particularly when it comes to customer interaction. In many businesses, customer service kiosks, automated check-ins, and digital interfaces handle basic transactions. However, customers expect a warm, personalised interaction from employees when dealing with more complex issues. The ability to seamlessly blend efficiency with genuine customer care is highly valued.

**Tip**: When working with technology-driven systems, find moments to add a personal touch. For example, if you work in a customer-facing role, make sure that automated services don't replace basic courtesies. Adding simple gestures, like a friendly greeting or follow-up question, will show that you respect the balance between efficiency and humanity that Japanese companies strive to maintain.

# Learn the Basics of Robotics if You're in a Tech-Heavy Industry

JAPAN LEADS THE WORLD in robotics, and if you're in industries like manufacturing, healthcare, or retail, chances are you'll interact with or even operate robotic systems. Some companies use robotic exoskeletons to assist employees with physical tasks, while others rely on robots to handle repetitive work. While you don't need to be an expert in robotics, having a basic understanding of the technology can make your job easier and demonstrate that you're committed to learning Japan's unique business tools.

**Tip**: If possible, ask for an introduction to the robotic systems used in your workplace. Many companies offer orientation sessions or on-the-job training to help employees get comfortable with robotics. Showing interest and developing a working knowledge of these systems will allow you to navigate tech-heavy environments more comfortably.

# Understand That Efficiency Isn't Just Technology—It's a Mindset

IN JAPAN, EFFICIENCY is a deeply ingrained value that goes beyond technology. Employees are often encouraged to perform tasks methodically, minimising waste and avoiding unnecessary steps. You may notice that Japanese colleagues meticulously plan their day or approach even small tasks with a high degree of focus. This dedication to efficiency is part of the culture, and it applies not only to work processes but also to communication and collaboration.

**Tip**: Practice structured time management and organisation. Streamline your tasks and avoid taking shortcuts that could compromise quality. By respecting Japan's approach to precision and minimising errors, you'll not only fit in but also develop habits that improve your productivity.

## Know When to Rely on Automation and When to Be Hands-On

ONE CHALLENGE IN A high-tech workplace is knowing when to trust automated systems and when to take a more hands-on approach. While Japan values efficiency, the importance of human judgment is also recognised, especially in situations that require flexibility or sensitivity. For instance, while an AI scheduling tool might suggest the most efficient meeting times, Japanese teams often prefer to consider personal schedules to ensure harmony.

**Tip:** Balance reliance on automated systems with a personal, human touch. If an automated system suggests a course of action that seems insensitive or too rigid, don't hesitate to apply your judgment. This balance shows that you value both efficiency and the human elements that Japanese workplaces appreciate.

## Be Patient with Procedural Steps—Technology Won't Change Everything

DESPITE JAPAN'S TECHNOLOGICAL advancements, certain processes remain bureaucratic. Many Japanese companies still require extensive paperwork, formal approvals, and adherence to protocol, even if a digital alternative exists. It's a reminder that efficiency in Japan doesn't always mean a complete embrace of digital solutions.

**Tip:** Accept that some processes may feel slow or overly procedural, even in a tech-savvy workplace. Rather than viewing it as inefficiency, approach these steps as part of Japan's structured way of doing business. Knowing when to embrace the process, rather than resisting it, will save you frustration and help you adapt.

In Japan's evolving workplace, efficiency has become synonymous with technological integration. By understanding Japan's approach to automation, AI, and robotics, and adapting your own work habits to align with this culture, you'll not only become more effective in your role but also build a reputation as someone who appreciates Japan's unique approach to work. The key isn't just knowing how to use these tools—it's understanding when to blend technology with human intuition and respect for tradition.

## A Personal Note on Automation Overload

DESPITE THE PRACTICAL benefits of Japan's focus on efficiency and technology, I have to admit—sometimes, it feels like too much. For all the seamless operations and sleek digital processes, there are moments when I'm left wondering if we're losing something essential in the mix: the human touch. This sense is especially strong when I check into a hotel, only to find myself clicking through screen after screen on a kiosk, with a staff member standing silently by, watching me "click-click-click" through my check-in. At times like this, I can't help but think, *Why can't the staff handle this instead? Isn't that what hospitality is about?*

I understand the purpose of these systems: reducing errors, speeding up service, cutting down on costs. But something feels lost when service becomes so automated that the personal connection slips away. There's a balance to be struck here. Efficient service doesn't have to mean impersonal service, and yet, in many places, it feels like that's exactly what's happening. Automation has its place, but when it comes at the cost of genuine interaction, I can't help but feel like we're all being nudged toward a cold, transactional experience that lacks warmth.

In Japan's service industry—where politeness, attentiveness, and thoughtful gestures have always been hallmarks of good hospitality—it's difficult to reconcile this level of automation with a culture that values connection. I worry that if too many hotels, restaurants, and other service providers lean on these robotic systems, we'll see a decline in genuine service and humanity.

A part of me hopes that Japanese businesses won't let their staff "descend into robots" themselves, losing that spark that makes human interaction enjoyable and memorable. Efficient as it may be, service isn't just about getting things done quickly; it's about making people feel welcome, comfortable, and valued. As much as I appreciate the practical benefits of Japan's technological advancement, I hope that, as the years go by, there's a way to keep the essence of hospitality intact, ensuring that robots and automation complement, rather than replace, the human touch.

# Chapter 16: The Art of Playing Along with Robotic Staff – Patience as Power

In Japan, many employees—particularly in customer service and retail—tend to follow procedures so precisely that interactions can feel almost robotic. This isn't just limited to check-ins at automated kiosks; in hotels, offices, and stores, employees are often required to adhere strictly to scripts, creating interactions that may seem overly formal, rigid, or impersonal. For a foreigner, these interactions can be challenging, and the instinct to break through this layer of procedural formality can feel overwhelming. However, learning to "play along" can be both strategic and empowering. Patience, in this environment, isn't just a virtue—it's a valuable skill that can lead to smoother, more respectful interactions.

## Why Employees Stick to the Script

IN JAPANESE WORKPLACES, employees are trained to follow guidelines and maintain consistency. Deviating from these procedures isn't encouraged; it's often viewed as risking mistakes, and mistakes, in turn, disrupt harmony. For many Japanese employees, staying "on script" provides a sense of security and professionalism. They may be following a detailed manual that dictates exactly how they should greet, assist, and communicate with customers. While this system aims to ensure quality and reliability, it can feel restrictive to those accustomed to a more flexible approach.

**Tip**: Understand that the rigidity is cultural rather than personal. Employees aren't being intentionally robotic—they're following what they've been trained to do, believing it's the most respectful way to serve you. Recognising this helps to avoid frustration and to approach interactions with a bit more empathy.

## Patience as a Tool to Build Comfort

WHEN DEALING WITH ROBOTIC interactions, patience is your ally. By allowing the employee to follow their routine, even if it feels tedious, you're respecting their role and the expectations they're working within. In Japan, patience signals maturity and respect for others' efforts, even if those efforts seem overly methodical. Showing that you're willing to give them the time they need to "go through the motions" builds trust and encourages a smoother interaction.

**Tip**: When faced with procedural steps that seem excessive, remind yourself that patience can lead to better service in the long run. Allow the employee to work at their pace, and you'll likely find that they're more willing to help if issues arise later.

## Gentle Nudges to Humanise the Interaction

WHILE IT'S GENERALLY best to follow along with scripted processes, there are subtle ways to nudge interactions in a more personal direction. For instance, if a hotel receptionist is going through a checklist and the process feels overly formal, a simple, friendly comment or question—such as asking how busy their day has been—can often help break the rigidity. Japanese employees might not immediately respond with the same openness, but small gestures of friendliness can encourage them to step slightly outside the script, making the interaction feel more natural.

**Tip**: Try using small, friendly gestures to humanise interactions without disrupting the procedure. This can make both parties more comfortable and encourage a bit of warmth within the formality.

# Knowing When (and How) to Ask for Flexibility

IN SOME CASES, STRICT adherence to procedure can lead to impractical outcomes, especially in situations that require quick adaptation or problem-solving. If you need the employee to adjust their approach, it's best to ask gently and frame your request in a way that allows them to save face. A phrase like "Would it be possible to consider another way?" is less direct but still makes your needs known.

A friend of mine, who manages an international team in Tokyo, shared how he handles these moments. When faced with a particularly rigid process, he'll say something like, "Forgive me if this isn't the usual way—might there be any flexibility here?" This approach respects the employee's training while inviting them to consider an alternative. In Japan, framing requests delicately can make all the difference.

**Tip**: Use language that shows respect for the process but politely signals your need for flexibility. This way, you allow the employee to step outside the box without feeling pressured or embarrassed.

# Balancing Patience with Assertiveness

IN JAPAN, IT'S POSSIBLE to be both patient and assertive. While following procedural steps is appreciated, there are times when you'll need to assert your needs, especially if rigid adherence to the script is causing inconvenience. In these moments, maintaining a calm tone and respectful language goes a long way. If something needs addressing, it's perfectly acceptable to speak up, but do so in a way that maintains the harmony Japanese workplaces value.

**Tip**: Find a balance between patience and assertiveness by calmly stating your needs when necessary. Express your request politely, acknowledging the employee's effort. This approach keeps the interaction positive and ensures you're respected as well.

## Recognising When to Embrace the Process

AT TIMES, THE BEST approach is to simply accept the process and move on. Japanese companies often view procedures as a symbol of professionalism, and resisting them can sometimes cause more frustration. When the stakes are low, allowing yourself to go through the process, even if it feels excessive, can make the interaction smoother for everyone involved. Embracing the process as part of Japan's unique approach to customer service allows you to focus on the experience rather than getting caught up in minor frustrations.

**Tip**: If the process isn't causing a significant issue, consider accepting it as part of the Japanese experience. This outlook keeps things in perspective and can make for a more pleasant interaction.

For all its rigidity, Japan's adherence to procedural interactions is rooted in a cultural respect for precision and consistency. By learning to navigate these "robotic" moments with patience, subtle guidance, and gentle assertiveness, you not only enhance your own experience but also show an understanding of Japan's commitment to structured service. Ultimately, the art of "playing along" with robotic staff lies in knowing when to embrace the process and when to nudge it toward a more human touch.

# Chapter 17: Recognising (and Handling) Xenophobia in Subtle Forms

In my years navigating Japan's corporate landscape, I've encountered numerous instances where subtle forms of xenophobia surface, often masked by cultural norms and politeness. Understanding and addressing these nuances is crucial for any foreign professional aiming to integrate effectively.

## The 'Gaijin' Label

THE TERM "GAIJIN" (外人), meaning "outsider" or "foreigner," is commonly used in Japan to refer to non-Japanese individuals. While some may argue it's a neutral descriptor, its usage can carry exclusionary undertones. Being consistently identified as a "gaijin" can create a sense of otherness, subtly reinforcing the notion that one doesn't fully belong, regardless of how long they've lived or worked in Japan.

## Experiences of 'Hafu' Individuals

THE TERM "HAFU", DERIVED from the English word "half," refers to individuals of mixed Japanese and non-Japanese heritage. Despite their Japanese citizenship and upbringing, many hafu face challenges in being fully accepted as Japanese. A friend of mine, whose mother is Japanese and father is American, often shares stories of being questioned about her "foreign" appearance and being treated differently in professional settings. This highlights a broader issue of how Japan grapples with multicultural identities.

# The Toei Subway Banner Incident

IN OCTOBER 2024, THE Toei Subway displayed a banner featuring monkeys disrupting train services, intended as a lighthearted public service announcement. However, it sparked controversy due to its potential racial insensitivity, as monkeys have historically been used in derogatory contexts to depict certain racial groups. In the U.S., such imagery would likely lead to lawsuits under the Equal Protection Clause. This incident underscores the cultural blind spots that can exist in Japan regarding race and representation.

# Subtle Workplace Exclusion

IN PROFESSIONAL SETTINGS, xenophobia often manifests subtly. Foreign employees might find themselves excluded from informal gatherings or decision-making processes. I recall a project where, despite being the team lead, I was not informed about a crucial meeting. When I inquired, a colleague mentioned it was an "internal" discussion, implying that my foreign status rendered me an outsider, even within my own team.

# Navigating Subtle Xenophobia

ADDRESSING THESE CHALLENGES requires a nuanced approach:

1 **Cultural Sensitivity Training**: Advocating for workshops that educate staff on diversity and inclusion can help bridge understanding gaps.

2 **Building Alliances**: Forming relationships with open-minded colleagues can create support networks and facilitate smoother integration.

3 **Open Dialogue**: When appropriate, gently addressing instances of exclusion or insensitivity can raise awareness and prompt change.

**4 Legal Awareness**: Familiarising oneself with Japan's labour laws concerning discrimination ensures that one's rights are protected.

While Japan offers a rich cultural experience, it's essential to remain vigilant and proactive in addressing subtle forms of xenophobia. By fostering understanding and advocating for inclusivity, we can contribute to a more welcoming and equitable professional environment.

# Chapter 18: Navigating Relationships with Other Foreigners in a Japanese Workplace

As Japan opens its doors to more foreign workers, Japanese workplaces are becoming increasingly diverse, and the challenge of navigating relationships with fellow foreign colleagues has become more relevant than ever. While the shared experience of being a "gaijin" or foreigner can be a unifying factor, differences in nationality, language, cultural backgrounds, and work ethics can sometimes create tension. The added complexity of adapting to Japanese norms together, each in their own way, often highlights these differences. In this chapter, I'll explore practical ways to build harmonious relationships with other foreign workers while respecting the Japanese work culture that surrounds us.

## Embrace Cultural Diversity Within the "Gaijin" Community

ONE OF THE FIRST THINGS I learned was that the term "foreigner" encompasses a broad range of people, each with their own cultural context. Fellow foreigners might come from places as close as South Korea or as far as Brazil, each carrying unique expectations about work, communication, and personal space. Recognising these variations rather than assuming a one-size-fits-all "foreigner" identity is essential for building respectful relationships. For instance, a German colleague might favour a more direct communication style, while someone from Southeast Asia might prefer a gentler approach, often closer to Japanese norms.

**Tip**: Take the time to learn about your colleagues' backgrounds and communication styles. Small gestures, like asking about someone's home country or listening to their experiences, can foster mutual respect and create a strong foundation for collaboration.

# Communicate Clearly and Find Common Ground

LANGUAGE BARRIERS ARE inevitable in multicultural teams. English might serve as a common language, but for many, it's not their first. Misunderstandings can easily arise when communicating across different language levels and interpretations, so clear, straightforward communication is crucial. I've often found it helpful to confirm understanding in emails or meetings, even repeating key points to ensure clarity. This might seem tedious, but it can prevent bigger issues down the road.

**Tip**: When working with fellow foreigners, strive for clarity over brevity. Confirm key points in writing when necessary, and avoid jargon or colloquialisms that may not translate well. Simple, direct language is your best friend in a diverse environment.

# Respect Each Other's Approaches to Japanese Workplace Etiquette

JUST BECAUSE WE'RE all foreigners doesn't mean we'll all adapt to Japanese work culture in the same way. Some of us might feel comfortable with bowing rituals and formal greetings, while others may struggle with it. I remember when a French colleague expressed frustration with certain formalities, feeling they were unnecessary. Another colleague from Singapore, however, adopted Japanese customs readily, finding them similar to her own culture. The variance in attitudes toward Japanese norms can sometimes create friction, especially if one person's approach is seen as disrespectful or overly compliant.

**Tip**: Respect each other's ways of adjusting to Japanese norms, understanding that everyone is on their own journey. Avoid criticising others for how closely they adhere to Japanese etiquette; instead, lead by example and allow each person the space to find their own balance.

# Build a Supportive Network for Learning and Adapting

WORKING IN JAPAN OFTEN feels like learning a new language, both literally and figuratively. Forming a support network with other foreigners can be invaluable. I've found that sharing experiences—whether it's how to handle a procedural hurdle or what to expect during certain company events—helps everyone feel more prepared. My own group of foreign colleagues has been a lifeline during moments of cultural confusion, offering both practical advice and emotional support. We've navigated everything from complex holiday schedules to figuring out the subtle hierarchy in seating arrangements at meetings.

**Tip**: Create informal group check-ins or lunch gatherings to share insights and lessons learned. These moments of solidarity can boost morale and provide helpful tips on adapting to Japanese workplace culture.

# Address Tensions Respectfully and Promptly

CULTURAL AND PERSONAL differences can sometimes lead to tension, especially when working under the pressure of deadlines or performance expectations. Addressing these issues early is essential, as letting them fester can impact not only your relationships with other foreign colleagues but also your integration within the broader

Japanese team. For example, if a colleague's approach seems too abrupt or dismissive, it's often better to address it directly—preferably one-on-one, with respect and openness to their perspective.

**Tip**: When misunderstandings arise, avoid escalating them in group settings. Speak privately with the individual involved, framing your concerns as questions rather than accusations. This approach can help resolve conflicts without creating discomfort for others.

## Recognise Shared Challenges but Avoid Creating a "Gaijin Bubble"

WHILE IT'S NATURAL to gravitate toward people who share your experience of being foreign in Japan, it's also essential to avoid becoming too insular. Falling into a "gaijin bubble" can unintentionally isolate you from your Japanese colleagues and lead to a disconnect with the company culture. I've seen how easy it is for groups of foreigners to spend breaks or lunches exclusively together, which can sometimes create an unspoken divide between them and the Japanese team members.

**Tip**: Make an effort to interact with Japanese colleagues regularly. Whether it's joining a casual conversation or inviting them for lunch, small efforts to integrate within the broader team demonstrate that you're genuinely invested in becoming part of the workplace.

## Finding Balance in a Diverse Environment

NAVIGATING RELATIONSHIPS with other foreigners in a Japanese workplace is an art in itself. While we may share the experience of being outsiders, our approaches, expectations, and cultural backgrounds differ. The key to coexisting in such a diverse setting is to respect each other's unique perspectives, remain open to learning, and strike a balance between supporting each other and integrating into the Japanese environment.

In the end, working alongside other foreigners is a reminder of the globalised nature of today's Japanese workplace. By embracing both the commonalities and differences within this diverse group, you'll not only strengthen your own experience but contribute to a more inclusive and understanding work culture for everyone involved.

# Chapter 19: Conclusion

*W*akaru is not about changing the Japanese workplace—it's about learning to work with it. Understanding the hidden codes, the rituals, and even the hypocrisies allows a foreigner to navigate Japan's corporate world successfully.

You don't need to blend in completely, but learning when to nod along and when to stand your ground is essential. Use these insights as a guide not to merely survive, but to thrive, in one of the world's most complex and fascinating work cultures.